The Bottom Line

The Bottom Line

Business Finance:
Your Questions Answered

Paul Barrow

First published in Great Britain in 2001 by
Virgin Publishing Ltd
Thames Wharf Studios
Rainville Road
London
W6 9HA

ISBN 0 7535 0569 X

Series Consultant: Professor David Storey
Joint Series Editors: Robert Craven, Grier Palmer

Series design by Janice Mather at Ben Cracknell Studios
Typeset by Phoenix Photosetting, Chatham, Kent
Printed and bound in Great Britain by Mackays of Chatham, Chatham, Kent

Contents

Foreword
by Sir Richard Branson

It feels a bit odd to be writing a foreword to a business book. Perhaps it's because I haven't always done business by the book myself. Sometimes I've regretted that, and sometimes I've been glad that I followed my instincts instead of doing what conventional advisers might have recommended.

One thing I've learned is that there's no right way to do things in life. There is no 'magic bullet' for success in business. What works for Virgin Atlantic might not be right for British Airways; what suits your business could be completely wrong for someone else's. But any advice that can help you beat the odds and succeed in business has got to be a good thing. Listening to lots of people's ideas before taking a decision has always been something I have strongly believed in.

Every book in this series has been written by an expert in his or her field, and they've come up with lots of interesting and thought-provoking ideas. But the most important thing is to do what you personally feel is right.

Business should be fun. Enjoy what you do, and success comes within reach.

Good luck!

Preface

The Virgin Business Guides series has to have a book on finance . . . otherwise it couldn't consider itself to offer a comprehensive service to those owning and managing smaller firms.

The problem is that most such books are rigidly boring! Partly that is because, while we all know money is important, it is difficult to make it interesting in print. Somehow such books all seem designed for people either studying for, or who have passed, accountancy exams. They do not seem to be written for the Virgin Business Guides' target audience of busy non-specialists who want crisp answers to specific questions.

And. . . whisper it quietly. . . perhaps those attracted by the subject of finance/accountancy may not themselves be the most exciting of individuals!

So, a finance book, if it is going to be successful with our audience, has got to be doubly innovative to break out of the 'worthy but boring' format. Paul Barrow, known to the readers of this series for his *The Best-Laid Business Plans*, does this in four ways:

- Instead of dealing with issues in a chapter-by-chapter format, his style is to use the FAQ [Frequently Asked Questions] format.
- While Paul is a qualified accountant who has been a Finance Director of a quoted company, he is also an accomplished and experienced teacher to smaller firms here at Warwick.
- Quite simply, Paul Barrow knows what the FAQs are. He is also able to tell you what the answers are in a way you will understand.

The answers to the FAQ follow a consistent format, so the reader knows what is coming next.

Even so, the FAQ format does have its problems. The biggest is that it tends to be superficial. Too often the reader is left hanging at the end. Where do you go if you need to know more?

Paul Barrow tries to avoid this – although it is bound to happen to some extent in a book of this size. His strategy is to end with a 'Where can I get further help?' question. This points you to an associated or linked FAQ or tells you where to seek more information.

But if, as I expect, you are busy, why not get on with reading the text. I'm sure you'll find it of real value.

Professor David Storey
Director, Centre for Small and Medium Sized Enterprises
Warwick Business School, University of Warwick

Introduction

Most people who are involved in running businesses are not accountants (did I hear someone say 'thankfully'?). However, every day they are faced with making decisions that involve finance. They need quick answers to everyday business issues that affect the bottom line. So where do they go for this help? It would be nice to think that everyone has an accountant by their side 24 hours a day who can communicate in a non-technical manner. Unfortunately, this is not the case for most businesses. Most small businesses cannot afford constant access to an accountant. The other issue is that most business people think accountants speak a foreign language – there may be an element of truth in this.

Another option is to read a finance book to find the answers that you need. There is a whole range of books on every single aspect of finance – so there is plenty of choice. They are usually cost-effective – apart from some of the more esoteric works. However about 90 per cent of them are written by accountants or teaching academics, so they tend to be serious tomes. Their target audience is usually students studying for accounting exams as part of a professional qualification or degree course. Also, in most cases, the issues they cover tend to be quite narrow, so to cover most of the finance issues you may be interested in you would need several books. The way they are structured makes it difficult for the reader to dip into to find the answers they need. They are structured in chapters and not by specific answers to frequently asked questions.

This book recognises that business people want a book written specifically for them. They don't want to know everything about finance: they want quick answers to their questions. In general, they want to know how to make their businesses more profitable, to improve cash flow and to know how to manage their businesses better. This book will help you to achieve all this.

This book:

- Sets out as answers to specific frequently asked questions (FAQs) – this way you can get a quick answer to your question without having to plough through a chapter (or more) of a book.
- Is written for busy business people (not students) – so it cuts to the chase and only as much information as is needed to answer the specific FAQ (on average each FAQ is covered in about 1,500 words – many are shorter than this).
- Is written by someone who spends much of his time working with non-financial people – so it uses a non-technical approach, wherever possible, together with worked-out examples to explain things.
- Covers self-standing FAQs – so you get everything you need in one shot to answer your immediate question, without having to refer to another 'chapter'.
- The FAQs are grouped by common ground – for example the first nine are all about cash flow and short-term funding. If you read these you will know most of what you need to know about cash flow.

How to use this book

This is not the complete book of business finance – that does not exist and, if it did, it would be the size of the *Encyclopaedia Britannica*! However, it does focus on providing answers to the most frequently asked questions covering:

- cash flow and short-term funding
- profitability
- longer-term funding
- understanding financial statements
- business control
- buying a business

Each of the FAQs is self-standing and you will find all you need to know to deal with it. In some cases FAQs are linked and when you have read one you may want to read another. For example, when you have read FAQ 1 on understanding why profitable growth businesses run out of cash, you may want to read FAQ 2, which helps you to find out whether *your* business will run out of cash.

You will find that the FAQs follow standard formats for:

1. Business problems: e.g., FAQ 1: 'My business is growing and profitable, but why is it always short of cash?' The response to this and similar FAQs will be laid out as follows:

- **Why does it happen in the first place?** – this provides a short explanation of why and how the business problem occurs. It may also include an example with numbers to reinforce this.
- **What can I do to stop this happening?** – this offers a range of solutions to the problem.
- **What will happen if I don't do something about it (short term/long term)?** – outlines whether your business will survive in the short/long term if you ignore the problem.
- **Is there a quick and dirty fix for the problem?** – offers a range of easy-to-implement quick fixes (if they exist) to achieve short term survival.
- **Whose responsibility is it?** – says who is responsible for making sure the business gets out and keeps out of trouble.
- **Where can I get further help?** – offers some more useful sources of help. These could be other FAQs that you should look at, people or organisations that you can contact, or other books to which you might want to refer.

2. 'How do I?' questions: e.g., FAQ 21: 'How do I get the best price for my business when I sell it?' The response to this and similar FAQs will be laid out similar to this:

- **What do I need to know?** – outlines the issues involved in answering the question.
- **Specific suggestions** (which will vary in format slightly from FAQ to FAQ).
- **Where can I get further help?** – offers some more useful sources of help. These could be other FAQs that you should look at, people or organisations that you can contact, or other books you might want to refer to.

Do move around the FAQs in the order you wish, which will almost certainly be in the order of priority of problems. If you find that you have several FAQs grouped together – on profitability, for instance – then it may make sense to read the other FAQs on profitability and follow up some of the links to further help.

Finally, a few words of encouragement. You either manage your own or someone else's business, which means that you have already achieved a lot. Probably your main skills and expertise lie in sales, marketing, production, customer service or general management. Finance is a secondary, albeit important, responsibility – so you are not expected to be an expert in it. However, you can improve your financial capability and your business capability by addressing those problems and answering those questions that may be depressing the bottom-line performance of your business. Somewhere among these FAQs are the answers you need. I hope this book helps you to achieve more.

The frequently asked questions covered in this book

Questions on cash flow and short-term funding

1. 'My business is growing and profitable, but why is it always short of cash?'
2. 'How can I can I tell if my business will run out of cash?'
3. 'What is working capital – and why is it so important?'
4. 'How can I make sure my business does not run out of cash as it grows?'
5. 'How can I quickly work out a rough cash flow forecast without doing a proper cash flow forecast?'
6. 'Is it true that I could need nearly half my annual turnover just to fund my debtors and stock – and why?'
7. 'What is creditor strain and why could it ruin my business?'
8. 'My bank manager won't lend me any more money because my gearing is too high – what is this and what can I do to sort it out?'
9. 'My bank manager won't increase my overdraft – what other options are there?'

Questions on profitability

10. 'I have heard that knowing my break-even point is important – why?'
11. 'How can I use break-even to set profit objectives and selling prices?'
12. 'I've slashed my selling price and am selling more but I am still not making any profit – why?'
13. 'I've heard you can put up your selling price, lose customers and still make more money – is this true?'
14. 'I don't have an accounting system, so how can I produce a monthly profit statement quickly and cheaply?'
15. 'If I want to improve profitability and cash flow, what is the quickest way to do it?'
16. 'What is more important, profit or cash?'

Questions on longer-term funding

17. 'What is a business angel and where can I find one?'
18. 'I have got a great business idea but it's a bit risky – who should I go to for money?'
19. 'I have heard that venture capital is a rip-off – how do I make sure I don't get done?'
20. 'I am thinking of selling my business – how do I value it?'
21. 'How do I get the best price for my business when I sell it?'
22. 'If I take on an equity partner, how can I be sure they won't take over my business, and how do I get rid of them?'
23. 'What other longer-term funding options could be open to my business?'

Questions on financial statements

24. 'How do I make sense of the balance sheet?'
25. 'What does the profit and loss statement tell me about a business?'
26. 'What does the cash flow forecast tell me about a business?'
27. 'What is the difference between statutory accounting and management accounting?'

Questions on business control

28. 'How can using ratios help me manage my business better?'

29. 'What measures can I use to help monitor profitability?'
30. 'How can I control my working capital?'
31. 'How can I make sure that my business is still growing and that I am not taking undue risk?'
32. 'What are the key numbers that I need to know to control my business?'
33. 'How do I justify spending any money at all on capital projects that will improve my business?'

Questions on buying a business

34. 'How do you buy a business?'
35. 'How much should I pay to buy a lossmaking business?'
36. 'How do I make sure that there are no nasty surprises after I have bought a business?'
37. 'Which is easier/better: organic growth or growth through acquisition?'
38. 'How should I fund a business that I am buying?'

CHAPTER ONE

Questions on cash flow and short-term funding

 FAQ 1

'My business is growing and profitable, but why is it always short of cash?'

Why does it happen in the first place?

It happens to most high-growth businesses at some time in their lives, so do not feel as if you are on your own here. The three key factors that cause the problem are hidden in the question – 'growth', 'profit' and 'cash'. Any one or all of these factors could be causing your problem.

- **Growth:** If your rate of growth is high it is highly unlikely that your business will be able to generate cash fast enough to keep up with this.
- **Profit:** If your business has low profitability at the gross-profit and/or net-profit level it may not be able to fund any growth at all.
- **Cash:** It may be that your cash position is poor because you are being 'squeezed' by your suppliers, who want paying before your customers have paid you.

Your friendly bank manager has seen this situation more times than he or she cares to remember. It is euphemistically referred to as 'overtrading'. This term is used to explain the situation in which a business is growing beyond its ability to generate or get additional working capital (cash). In simple terms, this is what happens.

Stage 1 (good news?): The business experiences sales growth.

Stage 2 (cash goes out of the business): To meet these extra sales the business buys more stock and increases production, which results in higher running costs and higher levels of work in progress and finished stocks. Some of this has to be paid for almost immediately (wages and salaries), while the rest can be obtained on normal credit terms (say 30 days).

Stage 3 (cash continues to go out of the business): As sales grow, there is no immediate improvement in cash coming into the business because the new sales are given either normal or extended credit terms (say 60 days by the time you have collected and banked it). At the same time, more stock is still being bought (and paid for), as are wages and salaries.

Stage 4 (some cash starts to come in but even more cash is going out): At last some cash is coming in from sales made in earlier months, but even more cash is needed for stock, wages and salaries to meet the higher level of sales being made (but not paid for).

Summary: The resulting effect is that, while profitability has improved, the cash position has got worse.

An example with some numbers

Let's look at an example with some numbers to highlight how a profitable business might look before and during a period of high growth. First, let's see how the profit statement looks for a business making steady sales of £10,000 every month – we have shown the figures for the last six months of their financial year:

Steady state – no growth						
Profit statement						
	Month 7	Month 8	Month 9	Month 10	Month 11	Month 12
Sales	10,000	10,000	10,000	10,000	10,000	10,000
Cost of sales:						
Materials	5,000	5,000	5,000	5,000	5,000	5,000
Wages	3,000	3,000	3,000	3,000	3,000	3,000
	8,000	8,000	8,000	8,000	8,000	8,000
Gross profit	2,000	2,000	2,000	2,000	2,000	2,000

Profit statement – *continued*

	Month 7	Month 8	Month 9	Month 10	Month 11	Month 12
Overheads:						
Salaries	750	750	750	750	750	750
Rent, rates etc.	250	250	250	250	250	250
Advertising	150	150	150	150	150	150
Repairs and maintenance	100	100	100	100	100	100
	1,250	1,250	1,250	1,250	1,250	1,250
Net profit	750	750	750	750	750	750
Net profit – year to date	750	1,500	2,250	3,000	3,750	4,500

In the above example, we see a very healthy profit of £750 per month, giving a cumulative profit of £4,500 (6 × £750) after 6 months. So far, so good – steady business with steady profits. But how might the cash flow look for this same business? This is shown below:

Cash flow statement

	Month 7	Month 8	Month 9	Month 10	Month 11	Month 12
Receipts:						
Cash from debtors (60 days' credit)	**10,000**	**10,000**	10,000	10,000	10,000	10,000
Payments:						
Materials (30 days' credit)	**5,000**	5,000	5,000	5,000	5,000	5,000
Wages (paid in current month)	3,000	3,000	3,000	3,000	3,000	3,000
Salaries (paid in current month)	750	750	750	750	750	750
Rent, rates etc. (paid in current month)	250	250	250	250	250	250
Advertising (paid in current month)	150	150	150	150	150	150
Repairs and maintenance (30 days' credit)	**100**	100	100	100	100	100
	9,250	9,250	9,250	9,250	9,250	9,250
Net cash flow for month	750	750	750	750	750	750
Bank balance	750	1,500	2,250	3,000	3,750	4,500

Note: The figures in months 7 and 8 shown in ***bold italics*** are those cash receipts and payments that belong to previous months' trading. For example, the cash receipt from debtors of £10,000 shown in Month 7 is in fact the cash received from sales made in Month 5 (60 days earlier).

In this particular example the profit and cash flow figures are exactly the same because sales are a constant – £10,000 per month. However, add some growth, or in the following example some *high* growth, and the relationship between profit and cash changes dramatically. The example below shows sales growing by some £3,000 every month between Months 7 and 12, which equates to an average of 17.5 per cent per month during this period:

During a period of high growth

Profit statement

	Month 7	Month 8	Month 9	Month 10	Month 11	Month 12
Sales	13,000	16,000	19,000	22,000	25,000	28,000
Cost of sales:						
Materials	6,500	8,000	9,500	11,000	12,500	14,000
Wages	3,900	4,800	5,700	6,600	7,500	8,400
	10,400	12,800	15,200	17,600	20,000	22,400
Gross profit	2,600	3,200	3,800	4,400	5,000	5,600
Overheads:						
Salaries	750	750	750	750	750	750
Rent, rates etc.	250	250	250	250	250	250
Advertising	150	150	150	150	150	150
Repairs and maintenance	100	100	100	100	100	100
	1,250	1,250	1,250	1,250	1,250	1,250
Net profit	1,350	1,950	2,550	3,150	3,750	4,350
Net profit – year to date	1,350	3,300	5,850	9,000	12,750	17,100

As you might imagine, the above example shows a very healthy growth in profits in line with increasing sales – in fact the profit for the six months has increased by £12,600 (from £4,500 to £17,100). So far, so good – high growth business with high growth profits. But how might the cash flow look for this same business? This is shown below:

Cash flow statement

	Month 7	Month 8	Month 9	Month 10	Month 11	Month 12
Receipts:						
Cash from debtors (60 days' credit)	**10,000**	**10,000**	13,000	16,000	19,000	22,000
Payments:						
Materials (30 days' credit)	**5,000**	6,500	8,000	9,500	11,000	12,500
Wages (paid in current month)	3,900	4,800	5,700	6,600	7,500	8,400
Salaries (paid in current month)	750	750	750	750	750	750

Cash flow statement – *continued*

	Month 7	Month 8	Month 9	Month 10	Month 11	Month 12
Rent, rates etc. (paid in current month)	250	250	250	250	250	250
Advertising (paid in current month)	150	150	150	150	150	150
Repairs and maintenance (30 days' credit)	**100**	100	100	100	100	100
Total cash payments	10,150	12,550	14,950	17,350	19,750	22,150
Net cash flow for month	−150	−2,550	−1,950	−1,350	−750	−150
Bank balance	−150	−2,700	−4,650	−6,000	−6,750	−6,900

Note: As in the previous example the figures in *bold italic* are those cash receipts and payments that belong to previous months' trading.

Unfortunately, the cash position does not look so healthy – in fact it is worse than when there was no growth at all! At the end of the year the cash position has got worse by some £11,400, and, instead of £4,500 cash in the bank, the business has an overdraft of £6,900. Surely something is wrong. It's not with the maths, that's quite correct. The problem is all down to the fact that the speed of growth has been too fast for the business to generate cash.

What can I do to stop this happening?

The answer to the problem is to work on one or more of the three key factors causing the problem:

■ **Reduce growth:** If the business cannot borrow any more cash it should reduce the rate of growth to stop the decline in the cash position. In the example we have just looked at, the business should reduce its monthly sales growth from £3,000 to £1,000. (Please refer to FAQ 1 in the Appendix for profit and cash flow details.) Using this approach the six-month profit will be £8,700 and the year-end bank balance £700 (with a maximum overdraft of £50 in Month 9).

■ **Increase profit:** The most dramatic improvement in cash flow can be achieved by improving the profitability of the business. If the example business could reduce material costs from 50 per cent to 45 per cent of sales, and wages from 30 per cent to 25 per cent of sales, it could finance the original high-growth situation – assuming a small overdraft facility can be arranged. (Please refer to FAQ 1 in the Appendix for profit and cash flow details.) Using this approach the six-month profit will be £29,400 and the year-end bank balance £4,000 (with a maximum overdraft of £800 in Month 9).

■ **Improve cash flow:** If profitability cannot be improved and the business feels committed to an ambitious growth plan, the only alternative is to try to improve its cash flow by improving its credit terms – both to its customers and suppliers (if possible). In the example business, if it can persuade its customers to pay in 30 days it will generate very strong cash flow. (Please refer to FAQ 1 in the Appendix for profit and cash flow details.) Using this approach the six-month profit will be £17,100 and the year-end bank balance £8,100 (with a maximum overdraft of £150 in Month 7).

Finally if the business cannot improve its cash flow but still wants to go for an ambitious growth plan then it will need to find some appropriate form of finance.

What will happen if I don't do something about it?

Short term: If none of the three improvement options highlighted above is adopted the business will slowly run out of cash. It may be able to prolong its existence by selling assets to raise additional cash but it will struggle to continue trading as suppliers refuse to supply, because credit is withdrawn for non-payment.

Long term: There is no long term – the business will have run out of cash long before then.

Is there a quick and dirty fix for the problem?

Yes. Assuming none of the three proper improvement options can be adopted immediately the business can adopt short-term survival tactics, which could include:

■ slowing down payments to suppliers by legitimate or non-legitimate methods

■ getting to work on some of those customers to persuade them to pay more quickly

Whose responsibility is it?

Setting growth targets, selling prices and credit terms is a senior management responsibility. Improving profitability is every employee's responsibility. Very quickly the finance director or MD/owner must establish what level of growth can be funded and cut back growth to this level. Alternatively, fresh funding must be injected.

Where can I get further help?

You should look at the following:

> ■ If I want to improve profitability and cash flow, what is the quickest way to do it? (FAQ 15)
>
> ■ How can I tell if my business will run out of cash? (FAQ 2)
>
> ■ My bank manager won't increase my overdraft – what other options are there? (FAQ 9)

FAQ 2

'How can I can I tell if my business will run out of cash?'

Why does it happen in the first place?

This is related to FAQ 1 in many respects, which explained why a business runs out of working capital (cash) during periods of high growth. However, other businesses can and do run out of working capital – so how can it be prevented? The answer is to make sure that the ability of the business to generate cash is greater than its need to consume cash. Sounds like common sense, but what exactly is meant by this? It means that every day a business must be making enough net profit to fund its net working capital requirements – such as debtors, stock and work in progress, less any support it can get from trade creditors and the bank (or owners).

An example with some numbers

Let's have a look at an example with some numbers to highlight how a business can work out what its net working capital requirement is – and then do something about it.

Calculating how much cash a business can generate

In the example below we can see that net profit is 10 per cent of sales. This figure of 10 per cent represents the business's ability to generate cash (eventually) out of its profits. In arriving at this figure you can start with profit (as per the profit statement) and add back all depreciation (which is not a cash movement).

PROFIT statement		
		12 months
Sales		150,000
Cost of sales:		
Materials	50.00%	75,000
Wages	30.00%	45,000
		120,000
Gross profit	20.00%	30,000
Overheads:		
Salaries		9,000
Rent, rates etc.		3,000
Advertising		1,800
Repairs and maintenance		1,200
	10.00%	15,000
Net profit	10.00%	15,000

Calculating how much cash a business needs

So how much cash does it need to cover its net working capital requirement? The balance sheet extract below shows us the detail of where the cash is needed. We can see that, because its customers take 60 days to pay and it holds 60 days' worth of stock and work in progress (WIP), it has some £37,500 cash tied up in funding these. If we express each of these as a percentage of sales we can see the working capital requirement as a percentage of sales. Thus we can see that for every £1 of sales we need 16.67 per cent (or 16.67p) to fund debtors and 8.33 per cent (or 8.33p) to fund stock and WIP. In this example the business needs 25 per cent (16.67 per cent + 8.33 per cent) from each pound of sale to cover its working capital.

Fortunately, because this business can obtain 30 days' credit from some of its suppliers (materials, and repairs and maintenance) it is able to 'subsidise' the working capital requirement by 4.23 per cent (or 4.23p). Also, the bank (or the owner of the business) has provided cash that equates to 6.67 per cent (or 6.67p). In total, the working capital requirement has been covered by 10.90 per cent (4.23 per cent + 6.67 per cent).

Balance sheet (extract)		Year end
Debtors (60 days)	16.67%	25,000
Stock and WIP (60 days)	8.33%	12,500
Trade creditors (30 days)	−4.23%	−6,350
NBank/owners support	−6.67%	−10,000
Net working capital required	14.10%	21,150
Net working capital deficit	−4.10%	−6,150

Calculating the cash deficit

If we take this into account, the net working capital (cash) required by this business is 14.10 per cent (25 per cent − 10.90 per cent) of sales. Unfortunately, the business (as we saw earlier) can generate only 10 per cent of this – so there is a net working capital deficit of 4.10 per cent (14.10 per cent − 10 per cent). In layman's terms this means that the business does not have the ability to generate enough cash to cover its consumption of cash.

What can I do to stop this happening?

The answer is really quite simple and partially covered in FAQ 1. There are two prime options:

1. **Improve the business's ability to generate cash**: Essentially this means improving profitability, which can be done through: improving gross profit, reducing costs. In the example above, if net profit can be improved to better than 14.10 per cent of sales, the business will be self-financing.
2. **Reduce the business's need to consume cash**: Essentially this means improving cash management, which can be done through: collecting debtor cash more quickly, reducing stock holding, slowing down payment to suppliers (trade creditors). In the above example, if the business can reduce the net working capital requirement to below 10 per cent (the level it can generate), then the business will be self-financing.

What will happen if I don't do something about it?

Short term: If neither of the two improvement options highlighted above is adopted, the business will slowly run out of cash. It may be able to prolong its existence by selling assets to raise additional cash but it will struggle to continue trading as suppliers refuse to supply because credit is withdrawn for non-payment.

Long term: There is no long term – the business will have run out of cash long before then.

Is there a quick and dirty fix for the problem?

If (as in FAQ 1) the problem is being brought about by rapid growth, the most sensible solution is to stop growth immediately to get into a steady state.

> ■ Put up selling prices, which will improve profitability (and quite soon cash generation) and will slow down growth.
> ■ Put into place a severe cost-reduction programme and get to work on those debtors and stock.

Whose responsibility is it?

Senior management must determine the pricing policy and implement the severe cost-reduction programme. Very quickly the finance director, or MD/owner, must find out the business's ability to generate cash and get cash consumption in line with this.

Where can I get further help?

You should look at the following:

> ■ My business is growing and profitable but how come it's always short of cash? (FAQ 1)
> ■ How can I control my working capital? (FAQ 30)
> ■ If I want to improve profitability and cash flow, what is the quickest way to do it? (FAQ 15)

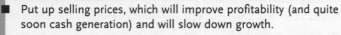

FAQ 3

'What is working capital – and why is it so important?'

What is it?

Without going into a detailed explanation of the balance sheet (that comes in FAQ 24), let us say that a business acquires short-term assets (called current assets), which are turned over fairly quickly in the course of business. They include raw materials, work in progress (WIP), finished goods, debtors and cash. However it also uses short-term loans (called current liabilities) to subsidise these. They include creditors and overdrafts. The net of these two is called working capital or net current assets. As a business grows, the increased level of trading usually leads to an increase in working capital needed. The need for working capital is further increased in a business with poor profitability – businesses with higher profitability can fund more of their own working capital.

The diagram below shows how working capital flows into and out of a business in what we call the **working capital cycle**. The example shown is for a manufacturing business, but the principle holds good for any type of business.

■ The start of the cycle is when a business buys in raw materials from its supplier to commence the manufacture of its product (or supply its service). If these are bought on credit then no working capital flows out of the business. However, the business now owes the supplier and this supplier has now become a creditor of the business. In effect this creditor is funding the working capital of the business on a short-term basis until it receives payment. If the business pays using its own cash, then it has used up some of its own working capital.

■ The next stage is for the business to convert this raw material into its own product and sell it to its customer. Making the product consumes further working capital (paying wages, rent, rates, heat and light etc.) while selling the product on credit does not bring in any cash straightaway to top up the working capital. However, the business now has a debtor who will in due course pay the business and thus inject additional working capital.

■ The next stage is for the business to pay the creditor for the goods that it bought earlier. This means more working capital has been used, and the creditor, by being paid, is no longer funding the business. To get to this stage the business has consumed considerable amounts of working capital.

■ The final stage is when the customer (debtor) pays for the goods. At last the business receives additional working capital and the whole cycle can commence again.

The working capital cycle may be quite long and can typically be up to three months for an engineering business. It is probably easiest to think of a working capital reservoir being topped up by cash coming from debtors and drained by all the other business activities.

The working capital cycle

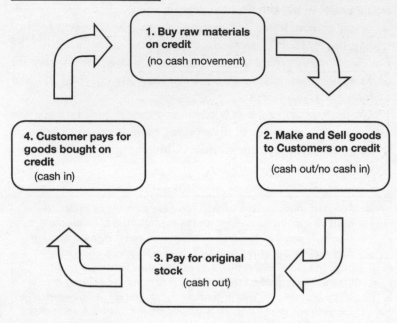

Why is it important?

Working capital is the lifeblood of a business and shows its ability to pay its bills (short-term liabilities) as they become due. Ideally, a business should have sufficient short-term assets (current assets) to cover its short-term liabilities (current liabilities). This ability to pay can be measured using the current ratio shown below:

$$\text{Current Ratio} = \frac{\text{Current Assets}}{\text{Current Liabilities}}$$

Ideally, this value should be greater than 1 and probably closer to 2. However, there are some industries where a ratio of less than 1 is acceptable. A low value indicates that a business finds it difficult to pay its bills. Once it stops being able to pay creditors a business will be unable to secure further credit from them or potential suppliers. This ratio is covered in more detail in FAQ 30.

What will happen if I don't do something about it?

Short term: Most businesses go through a period where working capital is tight – they find it difficult to find the cash to pay creditors.

However, most profitable businesses will grow out of this problem so long as they do not aim for high growth.

Long term: If lack of working capital persists, it is a fundamental problem caused by one of the following:

- Underfunding – in the case of a new or young business.
- Poor profitability – in the case of a businesses of any age.
- Poor debtor and stock control – in the case of a business of any age.
- Historical losses – caused by one year or more of poor profitability.
- Using working capital for the wrong purpose – typically to fund fixed assets.

Is there a quick and dirty fix for the problem?

Address whichever of the above is causing the problem.

- Underfunding: pump in more of your own cash or borrow it if you can.
- Poor profitability: put up prices, cut costs to kick-start profit improvement.
- Poor debtor and stock control: if your customers are taking too long to pay you, get tough. If your suppliers want paying too quickly, threaten to change them unless they play ball. Buy stock only when you need it and in the right quantities.
- Historical losses: only a prolonged period of profitability will undo this.
- Using working capital for the wrong purpose: stop it immediately. If you need to buy fixed assets (cars, plant and equipment etc.) don't use your bank account if you need it to pay bills. Take out hire-purchase or a bank loan.

Whose responsibility is it?

Senior management must make strategic decisions that are within the capability of the business – realistic growth targets, margins, credit terms, investment etc. However, thereafter managers are responsible for delivering it.

Where can I get further help?

You should look at the following:

- 1. What is creditor strain and why could it ruin my business? (FAQ 7)
- 2. How can I control my working capital? (FAQ 30)
- 3. If I want to improve profitability and cash flow, what is the quickest way to do it? (FAQ 15)

FAQ 4

'How can I make sure my business does not run out of cash as it grows?'

What do I need to know?

Any growing business will certainly need additional working capital (FAQ 1 highlights this fact) but it is also likely to need capital investment. It is unrealistic to think that you can grow a business to, say, double its current size without spending cash on additional plant, machinery, vehicles etc. It would therefore be foolish to start out on a growth plan that has no chance of success because the business will run out of cash. You can prevent this unfortunate situation from arising by working out in advance two key things:

- The total funding requirement.
- The additional funding required (over and above what you already have).

To calculate these you will need to know the following:

- the net working capital requirement at the new level of sales (for debtors, stock etc.)
- the capital investment required to achieve the planned growth (new equipment etc.)
- the business's ability to generate cash (crudely its net profit)

Now I suspect that you already have a good idea about most of these, especially if you have had a look at the earlier FAQs. Before you waste any time on a detailed monthly profit and cash flow forecasts, do an annual one to see if your proposed plan is 'doable' from a cash point of view. The starting point is your most recent profit and loss account and balance sheet, from which you can establish the current position.

An example with some numbers

Let's have a look at an example with some numbers to highlight how a business can work out what its total capital requirement is (you may recognise some of the numbers from FAQ 2).

This business is planning to grow from £150,000 (current sales) to £300,000 in 12 months' time. To achieve this the business will need to spend £25,000 on additional plant and equipment (capital expenditure) to give it the additional capacity to deliver the higher sales.

As a result the business will be able to generate future net profits of £45,000, as shown in the projected position profit statement below. Note that we have excluded any depreciation in this particular profit statement because it is not a 'real' figure and does not have any cash implication, which is what we are really focusing on here. The bank have promised to match the current level of funding at 10.77 per cent of turnover. The big question is, 'Will this business run out of cash if it carries out this plan?'

Profit statement		Current Position 12 months		Projected Position 12 months
Sales		150,000		300,000
Cost of sales:				
Materials	50.00%	75,000	50.00%	150,000
Wages	30.00%	45,000	30.00%	90,000
		120,000		240,000
Gross profit	20.00%	30,000	20.00%	60,000
Overheads:				
Salaries		9,000		9,000
Rent, rates etc.		3,000		3,000
Advertising		1,800		1,800
Repairs and maintenance		1,200		1,200
	10.00%	15,000	6.00%	15,000
Net profit	10.00%	15,000	14.00%	45,000

Balance sheet (extract)		Current Year end		Projected Year end
Debtors (60 days)	16.67%	25,000	16.67%	50,010
Stock and WIP (60 days)	8.33%	12,500	8.33%	24,990
Trade creditors (30 days)	−4.23%	−6,350	−4.21%	−12,400
Bank/owners support	−10.77%	−16,150	−10.77%	−32,310
Net working capital required	10.00%	15,000	14.33%	30,290
Capital expenditure required		0		25,000
Total funding requirement		15,000		55,290
Less: net profit		−15,000		−45,000
Additional funding required		0		10,290

At this new level of sales, its net working capital requirement will grow from £15,000 to £30,290. The reason for this growth is the continuing requirement to continue to offer 60 days' credit to its customers, and hold 60 days' stock and work in progress (WIP), while still getting 30 days' credit from some of its suppliers and having a bank overdraft of £32,310.

Add to this the requirement to spend £25,000 on additional capital expenditure and we can now calculate the total funding requirement, which is £55,290 (£25,000 + £30,290). Assuming that the projected net profit will generate cash of £45,000 during the year, the business will run out of cash. In fact it will need additional funding of £10,290 (£55,290 − £45,000). **A word of warning. The figure that you have just calculated is the average additional funding requirement** − it may be higher than this figure during the earlier months of your forecast period and lower towards the end.

You now know in advance that the business will run out of cash during the year and will not be able to fund the proposed capital expenditure. Armed with this information you can now decide what course of action to take before you commit to the plan. Can profitability be improved and debtor collection be improved?

What do I do with the information?

If you have done the calculation for total funding and additional funding requirement above you should have no excuse for running out of cash. The next thing to do is a monthly profit and cash flow forecast to see where the critical months are for low profitability and maximum additional funding (see FAQ 5). Armed with this information you can now put forward a case to raise the additional funding required. In this particular case, a term loan over, say, three years to fund the capital expenditure would enable the business to carry out the growth plan and remain within its current bank overdraft. A £25,000 loan over three years would cost about £9,700 per annum based on an interest rate of 10 per cent.

This would effectively take £25,000 off the total funding requirement (bringing it down to £30,290), which is more than covered by the reduced 'profit' figure of £35,300 (£45,000 less £9,700 loan repayments). If the business takes this course of action it should not run out of cash.

What will happen if I don't do something about it?

Short term: The business, while profitable, will constantly struggle for cash.

Long term: There may be no long term because without additional funding the business will be forced to cease to trade as creditors and the bank take action. The crunch time will probably come when the next VAT bill is due for payment.

Is there a quick and dirty fix for the problem?

If the level of additional funding required is quite small, say less than £2,000, then the business can adopt the usual short-term survival tactics, which could include:

- slowing down payments to suppliers by legitimate or non-legitimate methods
- getting to work on some of those customers to persuade them to pay more quickly

If the level of additional funding required is more substantial, then review the plan to see if the capital expenditure and growth can be phased in a more affordable manner, while still achieving as much improved sales/business performance as possible.

Whose responsibility is it?

This is the sole responsibility of the person at the top, especially if they make irresponsible growth plans without considering the cash consequences.

Where can I get further help?

You should look at the following:

> - 'How do I justify spending any money at all on capital projects that will improve my business?' (FAQ 33)
> - 'How can I quickly work out a rough cash flow forecast without doing a proper cash flow forecast?' (FAQ 5)
> - Read *The Best-Laid Business Plans* by Paul Barrow (Virgin Publishing, 2001).

FAQ 5

'How can I quickly work out a rough cash flow forecast without doing a proper cash flow forecast?'

What do I need to know?

As a starting point I would suggest that you look at the earlier FAQs on cash flow, in particular FAQ 4, which provides the basis for this 'short cut'. First, you will need:

> - a starting-point profit and loss account and balance sheet (ending just prior to the start of your forecast period)
> - a twelve-month profit forecast for the period ahead. This does not need to show the full detail for each month but it must show the anticipated sales for each month during this period

Using this information you should now be able to calculate a rough monthly profit forecast from which you can calculate a rough monthly cash flow forecast using the approach shown in FAQ 4.

An example with some numbers

Let's have a look at the same example we looked at in FAQ 4. We will look at this example using two different scenarios:

Scenario 1 (rapid growth)

The business immediately starts to trade as from Month 1 at an annual turnover of £250,000 (£20,833 per month). Under this scenario there is an assumption that there is an immediate market for the new sales, which may have previously been restricted by production constraints.

Under this scenario our example shows consistent sales and profitability in months 1 to 12 of the forecast period. The major change to profit and cash flow, therefore, all happens during Month 1. Using the same cost and cash flow relationships that were used when we visited this example in FAQ 4, we can calculate the profit forecast and cash flow forecast. The key points to note are:

1. Net profits are consistent at £2,917 per month.
2. Because annualised monthly sales are consistent at £250,000 the monthly net working capital requirement does not change.
3. There is a big increase in the net working capital requirement between projected Month 1 and the previous year of £20,833 – up to £35,833 from £15,000. This is due to the increase in sales, which means increased debtors and stock and WIP need to be funded, which are partially offset by additional trade creditors, which rise in line with this growth. It can be explained as follows:
   - Increase in debtors – £100,000 extra sales @ 16.67 per cent = 16,667
   - Increase in stock and WIP – £100,000 extra sales @ 8.33 per cent = 8,333
   - Increase in material purchase on extra sales for 1 month – (£100,000 × 50 per cent)/12 = 4,167

Balance sheet (extract)		Previous Year	Growth	Projected Month 1
Debtors (60 days)	16.67%	25,000	16,667	41,667
Stock and WIP (60 days)	8.33%	12,500	8,333	20,833
Trade creditors (30 days)	-4.21%	-6,350	-4,167	-10,517
Bank overdraft		-16,150	0	-16,150
Net working capital required		15,000	20,833	35,833

4. Thereafter the cash flow forecast shows (as you would expect) the net working capital remaining constant (in line with sales) and additional funding required falls as profits 'fall through' to improve the net cash in position.

5. The 'peak' additional funding requirement is £42,917 (Month 1), due to the rapid growth in sales and the £25,000 capital expenditure. It then falls to its lowest at £10,833 (Month 12). On average over the 12 months the additional funding requirement is £26,875 – a figure that corresponds to the £25,833 we calculated when we looked at FAQ 4.

(First 6 months):

Annualised sales	250,000	250,000	250,000	250,000	250,000	250,000

Profit forecast

	Month 1	Month 2	Month 3	Month 4	Month 5	Month 6
Sales	20,833	20,833	20,833	20,833	20,833	20,833
Cost of sales:						
Materials	10,417	10,417	10,417	10,417	10,417	10,417
Wages	6,250	6,250	6,250	6,250	6,250	6,250
	16,667	16,667	16,667	16,667	16,667	16,667
Gross profit	4,167	4,167	4,167	4,167	4,167	4,167
Overheads:						
Salaries	750	750	750	750	750	750
Rent, rates etc.	250	250	250	250	250	250
Advertising	150	150	150	150	150	150
Repairs and maintenance	100	100	100	100	100	100
	1,250	1,250	1,250	1,250	1,250	1,250
Net profit	2,917	2,917	2,917	2,917	2,917	2,917

	Previous year						
Cash flow forecast							
Debtors	25,000	41,667	41,667	41,667	41,667	41,667	41,667
Stock and WIP	12,500	20,833	20,833	20,833	20,833	20,833	20,833
Trade creditors	−6,350	−10,517	−10,517	−10,517	−10,517	−10,517	−10,517
Bank overdraft	−16,150	−16,150	−16,150	−16,150	−16,150	−16,150	−16,150
Net working capital required	15,000	35,833	35,833	35,833	35,833	35,833	35,833
+/(−) Net working capital	0	20,833	0	0	0	0	0
Capital expenditure	0	25,000	0	0	0	0	0
Less: net profit	−15,000	−2,917	−2,917	−2,917	−2,917	−2,917	−2,917
Net cash (in)/out	0	42,917	−2,917	−2,917	−2,917	−2,917	−2,917
Additional funding required	0	42,917	40,000	37,083	34,167	31,250	28,333

(Second 6 months):

| Annualised sales | 250,000 | 250,000 | 250,000 | 250,000 | 250,000 | 250,000 | |

Profit forecast

	Month 7	Month 8	Month 9	Month 10	Month 11	Month 12	Total
Sales	20,833	20,833	20,833	20,833	20,833	20,833	250,000
Cost of sales:							
Materials	10,417	10,417	10,417	10,417	10,417	10,417	125,000
Wages	6,250	6,250	6,250	6,250	6,250	6,250	75,000
	16,667	16,667	16,667	16,667	16,667	16,667	200,000
Gross profit	4,167	4,167	4,167	4,167	4,167	4,167	50,000
Overheads:							
Salaries	750	750	750	750	750	750	9,000
Rent, rates etc.	250	250	250	250	250	250	3,000
Advertising	150	150	150	150	150	150	1,800
Repairs and maintenance	100	100	100	100	100	100	1,200
	1,250	1,250	1,250	1,250	1,250	1,250	15,000
Net profit	2,917	2,917	2,917	2,917	2,917	2,917	35,000

Cash flow forecast

Debtors	41,667	41,667	41,667	41,667	41,667	41,667	41,667
Stock and WIP	20,833	20,833	20,833	20,833	20,833	20,833	20,833
Trade creditors	−10,517	−10,517	−10,517	−10,517	−10,517	−10,517	−10,517
Bank overdraft	−16,150	−16,150	−16,150	−16,150	−16,150	−16,150	−16,150
Net working capital required	35,833	35,833	35,833	35,833	35,833	35,833	35,833
+/(−) Net working capital	0	0	0	0	0	0	20,833
Capital Expenditure	0	0	0	0	0	0	25,000
Less: net profit	−2,917	−2,917	−2,917	−2,917	−2,917	−2,917	−35,000
Net cash (in)/out	−2,917	−2,917	−2,917	−2,917	−2,917	−2,917	10,833
Additional funding required	25,417	22,500	19,583	16,667	13,750	10,833	26,875

Scenario 2 (gradual growth)

The business has gradually to grow sales up to the new level of £20,833 per month. It will take time to generate the new sales and there will be maximum sales of £20,833 per month, reached in, say, Month 4, above which it will not rise, owing to the new production capacity restriction.

Under this scenario our example shows growing sales and profitability in months 1 to 12 of the forecast period. The major change to profit and cash flow is therefore 'phased in gradually' over the 12 months. Using the same cost and cash flow relationships that were used when we visited this example in FAQ 4, we can calculate the profit forecast and cash flow forecast. The key points to note are:

- Net profits are growing each month.
- Because annualised monthly sales are growing up to a maximum of £250,000, the monthly net working capital requirement is also growing.
- There is no big increase in the net working capital requirement between projected Month 1 and the previous year, owing to the gradual build-up in sales.
- Thereafter the cash flow forecast shows (as you would expect) the net working capital continuing to grow (in line with sales) and additional funding required falling as profits 'fall through' to improve the net cash in position.
- The 'peak' additional funding requirement is £37,100 (Month 3), due to the slow growth in sales and the £25,000 capital expenditure. It then falls to its lowest at £12,933 (Month 12). On average over the 12 months the additional funding requirement is £26,487 (very much the same as scenario 1).

You will find the full 12-month profit and cash flow forecasts (in a similar form to Scenario 1) in the Appendix.

Scenario 1 versus Scenario 2
In comparison to Scenario 1, Scenario 2 does not require as much additional funding (£5,817 less, in fact) with but by Month 12 requires £2,100 more additional funding. This really confirms the view that rapid growth (Scenario 1) causes far greater short-term cash flow difficulties than gradual growth (Scenario 2). However, over the 12-month period, the two average additional funding figures are remarkably similar: Scenario 1, £26,875; Scenario 2, £26,487.

What do I do with the information?

Use this information to work out how much additional funding you will need and when. If you need temporary funding – i.e. most of it is repaid within 12 to 18 months – then an overdraft is appropriate. If your additional funding need is hard-core (in other words, there is very little improvement over the next 12 to 18 months) then a term loan is more appropriate. Whatever you do, do not ignore what your cash flow forecast is telling you.

What will happen if I don't do something about it?

Short term: The business, while profitable, will struggle for cash.

Long term: There may be no long term because without additional funding the business will be forced to cease to trade as creditors and the bank take action. The crunch time will probably come when the next VAT bill is due for payment.

Is there a quick and dirty fix for the problem?

If the level of additional funding required is quite small, say less than £2,000, then the business can adopt the usual short-term survival tactics, which could include:

- slowing down payments to suppliers by legitimate or non-legitimate methods
- getting to work on some of those customers to persuade them to pay more quickly

If the additional level of funding required is more substantial, then review the plan to see if the capital expenditure and growth can be phased in a more affordable manner, while still achieving as much improved sales/business performance as possible.

Whose responsibility is it?

This is the sole responsibility of the person at the top, especially if they make irresponsible growth plans without considering the cash consequences.

Where can I get further help?

You should look at the following:

- 'What is creditor strain and why could it ruin my business?' (FAQ 7)
- 'How can I quickly work out a rough cash flow forecast without doing a proper cash flow forecast?' (FAQ 5)
- Read *The Best-Laid Business Plans* by Paul Barrow (Virgin Publishing, 2001).

FAQ 6

'Is it true that I could need nearly half my annual turnover just to fund my debtors and stock – and why?'

What do I need to know?

If you have looked at the earlier FAQs you should be aware of the fact that funding debtors and stock are two of the main reasons that businesses run out of cash. The working capital cycle shows us that a business has to buy stock and fund its sales for possibly up to two or three months (depending on the industry type) before cash starts to come in from its customers (debtors). However, because most small businesses are blissfully ignorant of how much money they are owed and how much cash they have tied up in stock, it often necessary to show them. They are not aware that an amount of cash close to the equivalent of 50 per cent of their annual turnover could be tied up in funding debtors and stock.

An example with some numbers

Let's have a look at the same example that we can use to illustrate the effect of funding debtors and stock. This business typically takes two months or 60 days to collect its cash from debtors. At the same time to ensure that it always can meet demand it holds two months' or 60 days' worth of stock. At first glance you may think this extreme but in some industries (typically engineering and print-related businesses) this would be considered to be running 'very lean'. Based on these figures this business needs just over 48 per cent of its annual turnover to fund just its debtors and stock!

Just to give you a bit more insight into the figures – so you can calculate these figures for your business (and give yourself a fright) the following assumptions have been made.

- Debtors are 2 months (60 days) = 2/12 annual turnover = (2/12 × 100 per cent) = 16.6666 per cent.
- Stock (raw materials): Based on raw materials being 40 per cent of the sales value and held for 2 months (60 days) = (2/12 × 40 per cent) = 6.6666 per cent.
- Stock (work in progress): Based on WIP being 70 per cent of the sales value and held for 2 months (60 days) = (2/12 × 70 per cent) = 11.6666 per cent.

Stock (finished goods): Based on finished goods being 80 per cent of the sales value and held for 2 months (60 days) = (2/12 × 80 per cent) = 13.3333 per cent.

It all adds up to a frightening prospect – especially if a business wants to grow fast. This particular business would need to find £48.33 of additional working capital for each £100 of new sales! If the business did not have the cash to fund this working capital it would need to borrow it.

How debtors and stock can swallow up cash

		% Annual turnover
Debtors	60 days	16.66%
Stock:		
Raw materials	60 days	6.67%
Work in progress	60 days	11.67%
Finished goods	60 days	13.33%
Total stocks		31.67%
Total working capital tied up in debtors and stock		48.33%

How do I calculate the 'days' figure?

You may be fortunate enough to be using accounting software that calculates debtor days for you. Certainly, most good accounting software will show the overall 'age' of debts as 'current', '30 days', '60 days' and '90 days'; or 'current', '1 month', '2 month', '3 month'. For the purposes of our days calculation we treat 30 days and 1 month as the same. However, you will probably need to calculate it and the example below will help you do this.

In this business the sales and debtor history is as shown in the table below. At the end of June the total debtors outstanding were £18,000, of which £10,000 represented the entire sales for June (100 per cent); £7,000 was still outstanding for May (78 per cent of that month's sales); £1,000 was still outstanding for April (13 per cent of that month's sales)

'Snapshot' as at 30 June

	Sales	Outstanding	%
June	£10,000	£10,000	100%
May	£9,000	£7,000	78%
April	£8,000	£1,000	13%
March	£7,000	£0	0%

Armed with information we can go on to calculate the June debtor days as shown in the table below. It is clear that, as all of June sales are still unpaid, then this debtor represents 30 days (or 1 month). However, the rest of the outstanding debtors figures are a bit more problematic. In total they amount to £8,000 (£7,000 + £1,000), which is less than the previous month's sales of £8,000 in May. For simplicity we say that the prior balance equates to 8,000/9,000 of May's 31 days = 89 per cent × 31 days = 27.59 days (which I have rounded up to 28 days).

Calculation of June debtor days		
Total debtors	£18,000	
Deduct June sales	£10,000	= 30 days
Prior balance	£8,000	
As the prior balance is less than May sales of £9,000 calculate as 8,000/9,000 of May's 31 days		= 28 days
	Debtor days	58 days

This takes care of calculating the debtor days figure – you can use the same approach for calculating creditor days. But how do you calculate stock days? Use exactly the same approach but substitute the stock figures for the debtor figures and cost of sales for sales.

What do I do with this information?

You use it to calculate your working capital requirements for your forecasts to make sure you don't run out of cash or to make sure you borrow the right amount. You also use it to prove to yourself (and others in the business) that you are taking too long to collect your debts and holding too much stock. When you have recognised the truth you can start to do something about improving the situation.

What will happen if I don't do something about it?

Short term: The business will constantly struggle for cash if debtor and stock days continue to be too high. You will take longer to pay your creditors in an attempt to conserve cash. If this continues in the long term your business will suffer from creditor strain (see FAQ 7), which will be disastrous.

Long term: If the problem of too much working capital being tied up in debtors and stock is not addressed the business will never be able to fund growth because sales growth requires too much working capital.

Slow or negligible growth will make the business vulnerable as it gets left behind by competitors. The business will not have cash to invest in new plant and equipment, new products etc., so it will miss out on new business opportunities. All in all, a crippling position.

Is there a quick and dirty fix for the problem?

Yes there is – lick your credit control into shape. Do all the right things, such as:

- Invoice on time: do it when the job is done, not at the end of the month (or sometime/never).
- Make sure your customers know what your credit terms are and start to chase just before an invoice becomes due for payment (not after – that gives them even more credit).
- Make sure you know your customers' internal systems for authorising and paying – you may be doing all the wrong things.
- Use your systems to the full to produce aged-debtor reports and follow-up letters.

As for stock getting out of hand, produce a stock report showing when each stock line was last sold and in what quantities. Use this to cut out slow-moving/obsolete stock. Match stock levels to reorder times (e.g., if it takes five days to reorder an item, just hold sufficient of that item to cover just over five days' production/sales. Obviously, be sensible, but utilising some of the just-in-time principles will help in the long run.

Whose responsibility is it?

This lies fairly and squarely with the credit controller (debtors) and stock controller (stock and WIP). Give them targets and monitor performance against these. Get rid of them if they are no good.

Where can I get further help?

You should look at the following:

- 'What is creditor strain and why could it ruin my business?' (FAQ 7)
- 'How can I quickly work out a rough cash flow forecast without doing a proper cash flow forecast?' (FAQ 5)
- 'If I want to improve profitability and cash flow, what is the quickest way to do it?' (FAQ 15)

FAQ 7

'What is creditor strain and why could it ruin my business?'

What is it and how does it happen in the first place?

You may have gathered by now that having adequate working capital is absolutely critical to the success of any business. After a business has done its best to improve debtor payment time and reduce stock holding, it may find it still has a gap in its working capital requirement. Often the bank may be seen as a logical provider of working capital – and in many cases it is quite right to use them. However, any business that buys in any products and services may (and should) be receiving credit facilities from its suppliers. We call this trade credit and it is a valuable and legitimate source of working capital.

The great thing about taking credit off your suppliers is that it is relatively easy to set up (fill in a few forms, and there are no interviews, as with a bank loan) and it usually carries no interest. Perhaps you can now see why it is so attractive. In addition, you can also 'hold on' to the money you owe to the VAT man, and the tax man for between 30 and 90 days. Between these two there is considerable amount of 'free' money that you can use.

However, if you abuse this source of credit and start to take longer and longer to pay your creditors, you will quite suddenly lose this facility. This is what is called creditor strain. It is that point at which you have pushed your creditors too far and they have withdrawn all credit facilities. Suddenly you will find that your suppliers want paying up front before supplying their goods. They will do this until you have regained their trust. The same will happen with VAT – you will suddenly find yourself being surcharged and moved from quarterly to monthly returns.

An example with some numbers

Let's have a look at the same example that we used in FAQ 6 to illustrate the benefit of using creditors to fund a business. Initially this business has made what I would call sensible use of its creditors to achieve about a 4 per cent 'subsidy' of its working capital requirement. At this point its suppliers are generally very happy because they are being paid on time – around 30 days. The VAT man and tax man are being paid on time.

Using creditors (sensibly) to fund your business

		% Annual turnover
Debtors	60 days	16.66%
Stock:		
Raw materials	60 days	6.67%
Work in progress	60 days	11.67%
Finished goods	60 days	13.33%
Total stocks		31.67%
Total working capital tied up in debtors and stock		48.33%
Less:		
Trade creditors	30 days	4.20%
Other		1.00%
Total creditors		5.20%
Net working capital requirement		43.13%

However, what if the same business were experiencing rapid growth and running short of working capital – what might it be tempted to do? I would expect it to try to delay payment to its creditors. You will have seen this as 'quick and dirty' fix in the earlier FAQs on cash flow. Let's see how pushing creditors can look very attractive as this business continues to delay payment to its own.

Below you can see the effect of the same business taking longer and longer to pay its creditors. To the business, there is something very attractive about squeezing its credit progressively further. You can see that if it can take just one month longer to pay its creditors it can reduce its net working capital requirement to just under 38 per cent. And if it can push out payment a further month it can reduce its net working capital requirement to just under 33 per cent.

Wow! What a success! The poor old creditors are funding the business (well, a lot of it).

Total working capital tied up in debtors and stock	48.33%	48.33%	48.33%
Less:			
Trade creditors	4.20%	8.40%	12.60%
Other	1.00%	2.00%	3.00%
Total creditors	5.20%	10.40%	15.60%
Net working capital requirement	43.13%	37.93%	32.73%
Payment	on time	1 month late	2 months late

Unfortunately, if the business succeeds in this plan, it will soon find that it has become very dependent on this source of funding – especially if it cannot get any more cash from its bank. This build-up of creditors is what we refer to as 'creditor strain'. Creditor strain is apparent when a business is takes too long to pay its creditors.

The crunch comes when these creditors have had enough of being paid late. The snap point can be triggered by all sorts of events, which may be outside the knowledge and control of the business. For instance, a supplier appoints a new creditor who has a purge on outstanding accounts. It may also happen as a result of supply shortages (remember the petrol shortages in the UK in late 2000?) which leads to supplies being available only to those who can pay cash.

The end result is the same. Suddenly all the creditor subsidy disappears. In the worst-case scenario if all credit facilities are withdrawn from our example company it will have to find a new source of funding the equivalent of 15.60 per cent of its turnover. That will mean it will have to find some £39,000 (15.6 per cent × £250,000) of new working capital from somewhere – and very quickly, too. This may be too much for this business.

A final word on creditor strain. Once a business loses its credit facilities it takes a long time to regain them. The likely scenario is that for some months it will have to pay cash and only after some months of 'behaving itself' will it be offered credit terms again. The message must be: push your creditors but don't push them too far.

What can I do to stop it happening?

The best medicine is prevention, not cure. A business must recognise when creditor strain is starting to occur. So how does it do this? Let's imagine that on average creditors required paying in 30 days. If they are paid dead on 30 days they will think the business is wonderful. If they are paid in 45 days they mutter a bit but will still do business. However, push payment past 60 days and in most cases they will have had enough and stop supplying. Of course, there may be some exceptions to this, depending on the industry sector. So if we know when creditor strain will occur how does a business spot it in time. There are two main ways of spotting it:

 Creditors days: Always keep an eye on your creditor days and see how this compares with your creditors' terms. If you have a computerised accounting system then it will automatically produce a monthly aged-creditor report to highlight those suppliers that you are taking too long to pay – the first signs of creditor strain. If you don't have automatic calculation of creditor days you can calculate it in much the same way as you can calculate debtor days (see FAQ 6).

■ **Creditor per cent**: If you do not have a quick way of calculating debtor days a rather crude way of getting to another 'warning sign' is to calculate creditors as a percentage of sales. In the previous example we saw that when creditors got to around 15.6 per cent of sales there was a problem. As a general guide you could say that if creditors remain below 10 per cent of sales there is not a problem. If they get to between 10 per cent and 15 per cent creditor strain may be starting to occur. Above 15 per cent and the business is certainly skating on thin ice.

As a final, less taxing way of spotting creditor strain keep your supplier statements. Most of these will show their terms and how old your debt to them is. Compare the two, and if you are paying them on average more than 30 days or a month late you are in danger of creditor strain.

Use any of these measures to avoid creditor strain.

What will happen if I don't do something about it?

Short term/long term: If you ignore creditor strain and all your creditors withdraw their credit at once, your business is in deep mire. Suddenly having to increase your business overdraft is not easy. Do not ignore creditor strain.

Is there a quick and dirty fix for the problem?

Possibly if you act quickly enough.

■ Recognise your key suppliers and pay them or strike a deal with them to secure supplies. If it has got to the stage where summonses are flying and winding-up petitions are being presented, it may be too late for any fixes.

■ It is possible to do what is called a creditors' voluntary arrangement, whereby you strike an agreement with all your creditors to pay them – either some or all of their debt – on an agreed basis.

Whose responsibility is it?

Senior management. Don't forget that creditor strain is an indication that the business is trading while insolvent: i.e., it cannot pay its creditors as they fall due. This is a criminal offence and directors have gone to prison for this.

Where can I get further help?

You should look at the following:

- 'How can I control my working capital?' (FAQ 30)
- 'If I want to improve profitability and cash flow, what is the quickest way to do it?' (FAQ 15)
- 'My bank manager won't increase my overdraft – what other options are there?' (FAQ 9)

FAQ 8

'My bank manager won't lend me any more money because my gearing is too high – what is this and what can I do to sort it out?'

What is it and how does it happen in the first place?

Banks, and I am not being critical of them, are in the business of secured lending. When they lend money they want it back, with interest and on time. They don't care if your business is having a bad year – they still want their money back. They are not risk takers and will actively seek to avoid it at all costs. As a consequence they have devised ways of looking at a business to identify how 'risky' it is so that they can decide whether to lend to it or not. One of the key measures (often referred to as ratios) that they use is something called gearing.

Gearing is a way of measuring the relationship between borrowed money (loans) and shareholders' funds (equity) in a business. So if a business has loans of £20,000 and equity of £40,000, it would be said to have gearing of 1 : 2 (£20,000 : £40,000) or 50 per cent (£20,000/£40,000). But why should the banks be interested in this breakdown? They see it as a measure of balance and commitment. Their view is that they want to be a minority partner in the funding of a business and that the owners of the business should have invested as much as they can afford (commitment). However, if the owners have put in as much in as they can afford the bank may then be prepared to match their investment (balance).

This means that in effect there is a cap on what a business can borrow. In general terms a business cannot borrow any more than its shareholders' funds (equity). This is what is known as 1:1 gearing.

An example with some numbers

Let's have a look at an example with some numbers to see how losses erode a business's ability to borrow. The table below shows a business moving from profit to loss and eventually back to profit again. It shows the effect on gearing of the five states shown below and its ability to borrow?

1. **The business is in a steady state:** It is profitable and the bank is prepared to make money available on a 1:1 basis, i.e., borrowings match total equity. Everything is hunky-dory.
2. **The business has started to make losses:** It has ceased being profitable and has wiped out all previous profitability (retained profits). Unfortunately, at this point the bank gets nervous and decides to call in some loans to maintain gearing. Just when the business really needs cash it has it taken away.
3. **The business plunges into serious losses:** Things get worse and total equity becomes negative, i.e., the shareholders have lost their investment. At this point the bank steps in again and calls in more loans to reduce what it calls its 'exposure', i.e., it implements damage limitation because it thinks the business is going to go bust. At this stage gearing has gone infinite.
4. **The business stops making losses:** Trading has improved but the bank is reluctant to help. The business, needing more money, is forced to take on a new equity partner; in other words, it has had to issue and sell more shares to raise cash. With this new equity, total equity turns positive again. The bank is now persuaded to restore some borrowing facility but because it is cautious it does not quite return to 1:1 gearing. It has returned to support the business only because it has seen other parties commit their money first.

5. **The business is making really good profits**: After a period of good profitability the bank is once more persuaded to restore 1 : 1 gearing and will make far more borrowing facility available than ever before. The effect of the additional equity injection has been to permanently improve the business's borrowing capacity.

Losses and their effect on borrowing ability					
	(1)	(2)	(3)	(4)	(5)
Share capital	10,000	10,000	10,000	10,000	10,000
New share capital				20,000	20,000
Retained profits	5,000	0	−20,000	−20,000	10,000
Total equity	15,000	10,000	−10,000	10,000	40,000
Borrowings	15,000	10,000	5,000	7,500	40,000
Total funding	30,000	20,000	−5,000	17,500	80,000
Gearing	1:1	1:1	Infinite	0.75:1	1:1

This highlights the tragedy that, as a business needs more cash because of losses, because the risk is perceived to be higher (using the gearing measure) the bank responds by reducing its borrowing – it actually calls in money. It is so governed by gearing that it restricts the availability of funding. This forces the business either to cease trading or find another equity partner.

What can I do to stop this happening?

The obvious answer is to ensure the business remains profitable. There are ways of legitimately keeping expenditure out of profit and loss by effectively capitalising it. This is called deferred expenditure and is used for expenditure on such things as research and development, brands, trade marks and property improvement.

If profits cannot be maintained then there is no alternative to bringing in additional equity. You will need to raise at least as much as the accumulated losses to restore equity to what it was originally.

What will happen if I don't do something about it?

Short term: Life will be very difficult – you will be ducking and diving.

Long term: There is no long term – your business will be starved of cash and die.

Is there a quick and dirty fix for the problem?

You will have to find a way of living without the support of your bank. In the short term this may be possible by delaying payment to creditors (if possible), persuading your customers to pay up early.

Find some short-term way to boost profits so that you can go back to the bank to show an improved position – even if it is just based on, say, three months' trading. This may persuade them to restore some borrowing facility.

Unless you can replace the bank with someone else, you will need to change your business radically. This may include reducing its size to improve profitability and reduce working capital requirement. At the same time you may need to sell off superfluous assets to bring in extra cash.

Whose responsibility is it?

Boosting profitability is the responsibility of senior management. Issuing new shares is a board and shareholder responsibility, which may have legal implications.

Where can I get further help?

You should look at the following:

> ■ 'My bank manager won't increase my overdraft – what other options are there?' (FAQ 9)
> ■ 'If I want to improve profitability and cash flow, what is the quickest way to do it?' (FAQ 15)
> ■ 'I have got a great business idea but it's a bit risky – who should I go to for money?' (FAQ 18)

FAQ 9

'My bank manager won't increase my overdraft – what other options are there?'

What is wrong with overdrafts?

It is interesting to note that most small and medium-sized enterprises (SMEs) in the UK use the overdraft as the central plank of both their short-term and long-term funding strategy. However, they are quite wrong to do so, and European businesses use a far wider range of funding options. The overdraft is appropriate only for financing working capital because it is in theory (and often in practice) repayable on demand.

There is also another downside to the overdraft: it is not very flexible because it is often set at a limit that is not high enough for many growth businesses. The chart below shows how this is graphically illustrated in a high-growth business that needs constantly increasing levels of working capital.

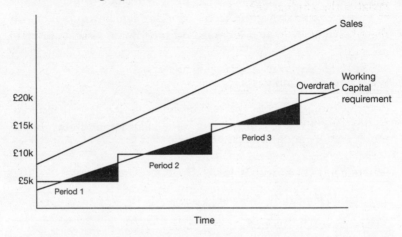

At the start of period 1 the bank has set a £5,000 overdraft facility. Initially this is adequate but as sales growth continues the business requires more working capital to support its increasing sales. The area filled in black between the stepped overdraft line and the straight upward working capital requirement line shows the extent to which the business needs more cash than the bank will provide. After some discussion the bank may increase the overdraft facility to £10,000 for period 2.

However, continued sales growth means that the working capital requirement once again breaks through the overdraft facility. The process repeats itself as the bank (this time far more reluctantly) finally agrees to increase the overdraft facility to £15,000 for the start of period 3. The bank manager can be heard to mutter the words, '... and this time you had better stick within your overdraft.' Unfortunately, the rapid growth continues and the business needs more cash. Very soon a £20,000 overdraft is required, which will not be sufficient for very much longer.

This constant back and forth to the bank to 'beg' for additional working capital/overdraft as the business grows cannot be the right way to fund this kind of business. What the business needs is a stepless funding facility that is constantly right for the turnover of the business. In effect, it needs a funding facility the same as its working capital requirement. But does such a facility exist? Yes, it does and it is called asset-based financing.

What is the alternative?

Asset-based financing is a funding facility designed to provide working capital to fund growing amounts of debtors and stock (exactly what the high-growth business illustrated above needed) and uses these only as security for the funding. It cannot be provided by your bank manager but it can be provided by a specialist part of your bank. In fact your bank manager will be only too pleased to put you in touch with them, if you ask. It also means that if you replace your overdraft with asset-based financing your bank manager will have to release any other security he may be holding – e.g., fixed and floating charges over fixed assets – because he is no longer funding your business.

The two main types of asset-based financing are:

> ■ **Factoring and invoice discounting** – which are similar in effect and enable the business to access up to 80 per cent of the sales invoice value of the goods sold within 24 hours. This means a business always has the level of funding it needs for the level of sales it is currently doing. The remaining 20 per cent (less charges) is paid over when your customer pays.
>
> ■ **Stock finance** – which in combination with 1 above can make up to 100 per cent of the sales invoice value available almost immediately. This type of arrangement can be very useful to businesses with seasonal demands.

For both of the above annual fees based on sales value are charged and vary according to the level of service bought, which can be very comprehensive. Interest is payable on the money borrowed at a rate that is usually slightly cheaper than bank borrowing.

How does it work?

There are subtle differences between factoring and invoice discounting and, depending on your business requirement, one or both may be appropriate.

Factoring

Using this, the business 'sells' its invoices to a factor (usually part of a bank) and contracts its sales ledger administration to the factor. This can include full bad-debt protection (called non-recourse factoring) or exclude bad-debt cover (recourse factoring). The former is more expensive because it covers an element of bad-debt insurance, so that the factor cannot have any comeback (recourse) against the business if the debt goes bad. Usually available for businesses achieving or forecasting turnover of around £100,000 or more per annum.

Invoice discounting

Using this, the business exchanges sales invoices for cash but retains full control over its own invoicing and debtor collection. However, bad-debt protection can be provided as part of this package. Invoice discounting will usually be the cheaper form of debtor financing if no other service is being used. Usually available for businesses achieving or forecasting turnover of around £750,000 or more (with no upper limit).

Stock finance

Using this, the business makes its stock available as part of an 'all-inclusive deal' with factoring or invoice discounting above to increase the amount of cash available against its sales invoices. This is in effect the sweetener to uplift the 80 per cent advance to 100 per cent of sales.

Is it as good as it appears?

In the past, factoring has had a bad name because business people usually assumed that if a business was factoring it had cash flow problems and was one step away from going bust. This was probably an unjust criticism of factoring, which has now matured, and has offered discounting (which is confidential) and does away with this problem – a business's customers do not know that it has financed its debts.

Asset-based financing has now come of age and is accounting for somewhere in the region of £70 billion of working capital funding in the UK alone. On this basis alone it cannot be ignored. In summary its pros and cons are:

Pros

- Flexibility – funding is always available in line with the level of sales, without preset limits.
- Improved cash flow helps the business to plan better and obtain better deals from its suppliers.
- Can be used either short-term or long-term.
- Factoring can in some cases be better and cheaper for a business than running its own credit-control department.

Cons

- External third-party credit control when using factoring (may upset some of your customers).
- Cost – because fees are based on sales value.
- Some types of business may not be acceptable.

Where can I get further help?

You should look at the following:

- Contact your accountant, financial adviser or the Factors and Discounters Association (020 8332 9955).
- Contact your bank manager.

CHAPTER TWO

Questions on profitability

 FAQ 10

'I have heard that knowing my break-even point is important – why?'

What do I need to understand first?

This is a fundamental question all about understanding profit and how it is (or is not) made. To many people profit is an accident of accounting. In other words, you add up all the sales for the month and take off all the costs and, hey presto!, a profit appears – or more likely a loss appears. In fact, the business of making a profit should be predictable. A business should be able to know with some certainty how much profit it will make for any given sales figure. Key to understanding how a business makes profit is to understand where its break-even point (BEP) is: the point at which total sales cover all total costs. According to Brian Warnes in his excellent book *The Genghis Khan Guide to Business*, the warning is that a company that does not regularly measure its BEP reduces its chances of success. It should also understand the dangers of having its BEP at too high a level of sales.

How do we calculate break-even?

Let's have a look at an example with some numbers to understand break-even. A business has just produced the following monthly profit statement. For simplicity it sells only one product and has a maximum capacity of 5,000 units:

Sales (4,000 units)	=	£20,000
Variable costs (materials)	=	£15,000
Gross margin	=	£5,000
Fixed costs:		
Rent, rates, etc.	£2,500	
Office salaries	£1,200	
Depreciation	£300	
Total fixed costs		£4,000
Net profit		£1,000

But what sales does it need to achieve break-even (cover total costs) and how do we calculate the BEP using the information we already have? A change of focus is needed. Start thinking about the profitability that each unit of sale makes and how many of these will be needed to pay for all the other business costs. Using this approach we can work out the following:

Unit selling price (£20,000/4,000)	=	£5
Unit cost (£15,000/4,000)	=	£3.50
Gross margin	=	£1.50 (or 25 per cent)
Fixed costs (other costs)	=	£4,000

We can now see that each unit sold generates £1.50 of gross margin or 25 per cent of sales. The next step is to calculate how much the business needs to sell to break-even, which we do as follows:

$$\text{Break-even point (BEP)} = \frac{\text{Fixed costs}}{\text{Gross margin \%}}$$

$$\text{BEP} = \frac{£4,000}{25 \text{ per cent}} = £16,000$$

This tells us that the business needs to make sales of £16,000 each month just to break even – i.e., cover all its costs. You may have noticed that I have slipped in a few new terms that you may or may not have heard of before.

Variable costs

These are, as the name suggests, all those costs that vary with sales: for each extra sale that is made some more of this type of cost must be incurred. Typical examples of variable costs are materials, direct labour (those people who make the product or service), sales commission (because it is based on sales made).

Gross margin

This is what is left of the sales price after all the variable costs have been taken off. Many observers regard gross margin (or gross margin percentage) as the most important measure of business performance because it represents the 'real' income of the business. Sales is a 'vanity' because it does not show the true gross margin income from each sale made.

Fixed costs

These are, as the name suggests, the remaining costs that do not vary with sales: if one extra sale is made no more of this type of cost is incurred. Typical examples of fixed costs are rent, rates, insurance and administration salaries.

What can break-even analysis tell us?

OK, so now we know at what level of sales break-even occurs, but what **profit potential** does this business have and how **vulnerable** is it? To show this, it is probably best to look at a graphical representation of the same information we have seen above over a range of sales between £0 (0 units sold) and £25,000 (5,000 units sold). The raw financial data is as shown in the table below:

Units sold	0	1,000	2,000	3,000	4,000	5,000
Total £ sales	0	5,000	10,000	15,000	20,000	25,000
Variable cost	0	3,750	7,500	11,250	15,000	18,750
Fixed cost	4,000	4,000	4,000	4,000	4,000	4,000
Total costs	4,000	7,750	11,500	15,250	19,000	22,750
Net profit	−4,000	−2,750	−1,500	−250	1,000	2,250

In the break-even graph (see below) we can see that fixed costs, which are £4,000 per period, are represented by the horizontal line going from 0 (on the left) to 5,000 units (on the right). To that has been added all the variable cost for each extra unit made and sold to arrive at the 'total costs' line. This starts at the beginning of the 'fixed costs' line (on the left) and moves upwards (to the right), ending at a value of £22,750 at the 5,000-unit point.

The final line represents the total sales, and starts at a value of 0 (bottom left) and moves upwards (to the right), ending at a value of £25,000 at the 5,000-unit point. You will notice that the 'total costs' line starts at a point above the 'total sales' line (at which point the business is making a loss) and crosses below at just past the 3,000-unit point (3,200 to be exact) – at which point the business starts to make a profit. This crossover point is marked with a vertical arrow (and BEP) and represents break-even for the business. After this point the business starts to be profitable because total sales exceed total costs.

Break-even graph

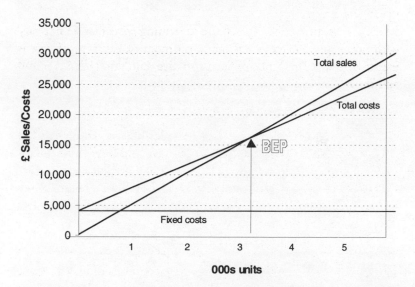

Suddenly the position of the business becomes very revealing. The graph shows that the business has limited potential to make profit – between BEP of 3,200 units and maximum capacity of 5,000 units. In percentage terms this means the business can only generate profit over 36 per cent of its production/sales capacity.

We also notice that, should sales drop by just 800 units from the current 4,000 units to 3,200 units (BEP), all the profits of the business are wiped out. The 'margin of safety' – the amount that sales can safely drop – is exactly 20 per cent.

In summary we can conclude:

- The business has limited profit potential.
- It is quite vulnerable to a drop in sales – in other words, it would cease to be profitable in a recession.

And what observations could we make on the following business using break-even analysis, which is currently trading at its maximum capacity/sales potential of 6,000 units?

Units sold	0	1,000	2,000	3,000	4,000	5,000	6,000
Total £ sales	0	5,000	10,000	15,000	20,000	25,000	30,000
Variable cost	0	3,500	7,000	10,500	14,000	17,500	21,000
Fixed costs	7,500	7,500	7,500	7,500	7,500	7,500	7,500
Total costs	7,500	11,000	14,500	18,000	21,500	25,000	28,500
Net profit	−7,500	−6,000	−4,500	−3,000	−1,500	0	1,500

And, when this is converted into a graph, it looks as shown below:

Break-even graph – high BEP

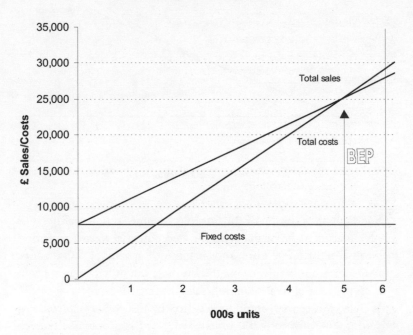

Once again the position of the business becomes very revealing. The graph shows that the business has very limited potential to make profit – between BEP of 5,000 units and maximum capacity of 6,000 units. In percentage terms this means the business can only generate profit over 13.33 per cent of its production/sales capacity.

We also notice that, should sales drop by just 1,000 units from the current 6,000 units to 5,000 units (BEP), all the profits of the business are wiped out. The 'margin of safety' – the amount that sales can safely drop – is 16.67 per cent.

In summary we can conclude:

> ■ The business has virtually no profit potential.
> ■ It is very vulnerable to a drop in sales – in other words, it would probably go out of business in a recession.

What can be done to reduce the break-even point?

If it is widely accepted that a business with a high BEP is a vulnerable business and has limited profit potential, then the challenge for every business is constantly to seek to reduce its BEP.

> ■ **Focusing on gross margin**: The greatest scope for reducing BEP lies in improving gross margin.
> ■ **Focusing on fixed costs**: Cut back overheads to reduce the vulnerability of the business during periods of uncertainty.

Where can I get further help?

You should look at the following:

> ■ Read *The Genghis Khan Guide to Business* by Brian Warnes (Osmosis Publications, 1987).
> ■ 'If I want to improve profitability and cash flow, what is the quickest way to do it?' (FAQ 15)
> ■ 'I've heard you can put up your selling price, lose customers and still make money – is this true?' (FAQ 13)

FAQ 11

'How can I use break-even to set profit objectives and selling prices?'

What do I need to understand first?

You need to have a working understanding of break-even – if you do not, please make sure you have read FAQ 10. Armed with this knowledge, you can see that the two questions in this FAQ can be answered using an extension of the break-even point (BEP) formula.

1. **Setting profit objectives**: Uses BEP as a starting point and then adds to this the profit objective (almost like an additional fixed cost) to arrive at the break-even profit point (BEPP)
2. **Setting new selling prices**: Takes into account the profit objective and calculates how this can be achieved by setting new selling prices even if sales volumes are projected to drop.

Let's look at a couple of examples with some numbers to see how we can answer these two questions.

1. How to use break-even to set profit objectives

A business has projected to make sales of £130,000 during the next financial year (5,000 units @ £26 each). On this basis a summary of its profit projection is as shown below:

Sales	£130,000
Variable cost	£85,800 (66% or £17.16 each)
Gross margin	£44,200 (34% or £8.84 each)
Fixed costs	£31,500
Net profit	£12,700

After some discussion the management have decided that a higher profit objective must be set. It has been agreed that the new profit objective must be set at £19,500. What is the new sales target needed to meet this new profit objective? To calculate this we use the following formula:

$$£ \text{ Sales target (BEPP)} = \frac{\text{Fixed cost} + \text{profit objective}}{\text{Gross margin \%}}$$

Which means for this example:

$$£ \text{ Sales target} = \frac{£31,500 + £19,500}{34\%} = \frac{£51,500}{34\%} = £150,000$$

To achieve the new profit objective of £19,500 the business has to achieve £150,000 sales. If you need convincing of this we can quickly show that £150,000 sales @ 34 per cent gross margin = £51,000 of gross margin. From this deduct £31,500 of fixed costs and – hey presto! – £19,500 of net profit appears.

2. How to use break-even to set new selling prices

Using the previous example again, the management have now decided that selling 5,000 units is not going to be possible in the current economic climate. It is agreed that 4,000 units is the most they can hope to sell and that has become the target. What must the new selling price be to achieve a profit objective of £19,500? Logic tells us that the selling price will need to go up, but what must it be? To calculate this we use the following formula:

$$\text{New selling price (NSP)} = \frac{\text{(Fixed cost + profit objective)}}{\text{Estimated unit sales}} + \text{Unit variable cost}$$

Which means for this example:

$$\text{NSP} = \frac{(£31,500 + £19,500)}{4,000} + £17.16 = \frac{(£51,000)}{4,000} + £17.16$$

$$= £12.75 + £17.16 = £29.91$$

To meet the new profit objective of £19,500 while selling only 4,000 units, the selling price must go up from £26 per unit to £29.91 per unit. If you need convincing of this we can quickly show that: 4,000 units sold @ £12.75 gross margin (£29.91 − £17.16) = £51,000 of gross margin. From this deduct £31,500 of fixed costs and − hey presto! − £19,500 of profit appears (again).

Understanding break-even is the basis for making informed decisions in a business. It is the cornerstone of being able to plan for profit − rather than its happening (or not happening) by accident.

Where can I get further help?

You should look at the following:

> ■ Read *The Genghis Khan Guide to Business* by Brian Warnes (Osmosis Publications, 1987).
>
> ■ 'I have heard that knowing my break-even point is important − why?' (FAQ 10)

FAQ 12

'I've slashed my selling price and am selling more but I am still not making any profit − why?'

What do I need to understand first?

The difficulty that many business people have is in understanding the intertwined relationship between volume, price and profit. If you change the two drivers (volume and price) just a little bit there will be a disproportionate change in profit. Understanding break-even is the starting point (see FAQ 10). The situation is made worse in low-margin businesses, where even a small reduction in price leads to a massive need for extra volume to generate the same level of profit as before. The problem is further compounded by business people who have a complete mental block and think that a reduction in price of, say, 10 per cent will be compensated for by an increase in volume of 15 per cent – it will not. In short, reducing selling prices will almost certainly devastate the profits of a business almost regardless of how much extra it sells.

An example with some numbers

Let's have a look at an example with some numbers to establish break-even and then see how reducing selling prices can have such a devastating effect on profitability. A business has just produced the following monthly profit statement. For simplicity it sells only one product:

Sales (4,000 units)	=	5,000
Variable costs (materials)	=	4,000
Gross margin	=	1,000
Fixed costs:		
Rent, rates, etc.	300	
Office salaries	600	
Depreciation	200	
Total fixed costs		1,100
Net profit		100

The initial observation is one of dismay – the business has made a loss of £100 even though it made sales of £5,000. What should the business do? The natural reaction is to suggest a course of action that will increase sales – which is what this FAQ is all about. The correct reaction is to do nothing until the business has first of all worked out what level of sales it needs to break even – i.e. to stop making losses.

So how do we calculate the break-even point for this business, using the information we already have? A change of focus is needed. Start thinking about the profitability that each unit of sale makes and how many of these will be needed to pay for all the other business costs. Using this approach we can work out the following:

Unit selling price (5,000/100)	=	£50	
Unit cost (4,000/100)	=	£40	
Gross margin	=	£10	(or 20% of selling price)
Fixed costs (other costs)	=	£1,100	

We can now see that each unit sold generates £10 of gross margin or 20% of sales. The next step is to calculate how much the business needs to sell to break even, which we do as follows:

$$\text{Break-even point (BEP)} = \frac{\text{Fixed costs}}{\text{Gross margin \%}}$$

$$\text{BEP} = \frac{£1,100}{20\%} = £5,500$$

This tells us that the business needs to make sales of £5,500 at 20 per cent gross margin each month just to break-even – an additional £500 per month over the current position. But in fact the need is £500 sales @ 20 per cent to generate the additional £100 gross margin to wipe out the loss.

Sound logic says that what is needed is a strategy to deliver just what is needed – protect the existing business and acquire just a bit more. The price-discounting approach flies in the face of this and provides an apparent solution that discounts the price (and therefore profit) generated by the existing business as well as the additional business it hopes to get. In effect it turns a small need for extra business of about 10 per cent (£500/£5,000 × 100) into a massive requirement.

Following our example a bit further, let's see what effect a 10 per cent reduction in the selling price will have on the additional business it will need (volume) to generate the additional £100 gross margin needed to break even. The table below shows how the business profits will compare for the three positions: original (before any price changes); proposed (after the 10 per cent price reduction); 120 per cent (demonstrating the extra sales needed to achieve break-even).

Effect of reducing selling price on profitability

	Original	Proposed	120%
Units sold	100	100	220
Selling price (per unit)	50	45	45
Variable costs (per units)	40	40	40

	Original	Proposed	120%
Gross margin	20.00%	11.11%	11.11%
Fixed costs	1,100	1,100	1,100
Break-even sales	5,500	9,900	9,900
Profit and loss			
Sales income	5,000	4,500	9,900
Variable costs	4,000	4,000	8,800
Gross margin	1,000	500	1,100
Fixed costs	1,100	1,100	1,100
Net profit	−100	−600	0

The immediate effect of reducing the selling price by just 10 per cent is to reduce the gross margin from 20 per cent down to 11.11 per cent on *every sale* made. If the business were to sell no more, then it would generate a loss of £600, which is what will happen during the period before extra sales volume is generated. Eventually, the result is that for just a 10 per cent reduction in selling price this business must more than double its sales (120 per cent) just to achieve an additional £100 of gross margin!

The clear message must be: **do not discount selling prices** unless it is for a limited period and for a clear purpose (e.g., for a period of time to drive out a competitor).

The price-reduction 'ready reckoner' shown below will enable you to evaluate the effect of price discounting at different margin levels. If our example business reduces its selling price by 10 per cent (read along the left-hand scale) for a given gross margin of 20 per cent (read along the top scale), then where these meet (highlighted square) indicates that a 100 per cent increase in sales volume will be needed just to stand still!

Price-reduction 'ready reckoner'

		Existing gross margins %								
		5	10	15	20	25	30	35	40	50
	2	67	25	15	11	9	7	6	5	4
%	3	150	43	25	18	14	11	9	8	6
Price	4	400	67	36	25	19	15	13	11	9
reduction	5		100	50	33	25	20	17	14	11
	7.5		300	100	60	43	33	27	23	18
	10			200	100	67	50	40	33	25
	15				300	150	100	75	60	43

% Volume of extra sales required 'to stand still'

What can I do to improve profitability?

The sensible answer is not to reduce (discount) selling prices, especially if the business has low gross margins. The business should adopt a plan to reduce break-even, which typically involves improving gross margin (by reducing variable cost) and reducing fixed costs.

Where can I get further help?

You should look at the following:

> - Read *The Genghis Khan Guide to Business* by Brian Warnes (Osmosis Publications, 1987).
> - 'If I want to improve profitability and cash flow, what is the quickest way to do it?' (FAQ 15)
> - 'I've heard you can put up your selling price, lose customers and still make more money – is this true?' (FAQ 13)

FAQ 13

'I've heard you can put up your selling price, lose customers and still make more money – is this true?'

What do I need to understand first?

Once again, understanding break-even (FAQ 10) is key to making sense of this conundrum. In fact increasing selling price while allowing sales volume to drop is a recognised strategy for low-profit businesses that cannot fund growth. Both profitability and cash flow can be improved by sensible use of this strategy. In effect, the explanation of this FAQ is the opposite of FAQ 12 (the effect of price reduction). This strategy can be very effective in low-margin businesses, where a small increase in price accompanied by a small reduction in volume can lead to a disproportionate improvement in profits being generated. The real beauty of this strategy is that, owing to the reduced volume of sales needed to improve profitability, the working capital required to fund debtors and stock is also reduced.

An example with some numbers

Let's have a look at the same example that we used in FAQ 12 with some numbers to see how increasing selling prices can have such a beneficial effect on profitability. The table below shows how the business profits will compare for the four positions – original (before any price changes); proposed (after a 10 per cent price increase); –33 per cent (demonstrating the reduction in sales it can suffer to be no worse off); –25 per cent (demonstrating how profits would increase if sales fell by only 25 per cent).

Effect of increasing selling price on profitability				
	Original	Proposed	–33%	–25%
Units sold	100	100	66.67	75
Selling price (per unit)	50	55	55	55
Variable costs (per units)	40	40	40	40
Gross margin	20.00%	27.27%	27.27%	27.27%
Fixed costs	1,100	1,100	1,100	1,100
Break-even sales	5,500	4,033	4,033	4,033
Profit and loss				
Sales income	5,000	5,500	3,667	4,125
Variable costs	4,000	4,000	2,667	3,000
Gross margin	1,000	1,500	1,000	1,125
Fixed costs	1,100	1,100	1,100	1,100
Net profit	–100	400	–100	25

The immediate effect of increasing the selling price by just 10 per cent is to increase the gross margin from 20 per cent to 27.27 per cent on every sale made. The result is that for just a 10 per cent increase in selling price profits will go up to £400 as long as sales volume does not fall.

Of course, sales volume may fall and, assuming it does not fall by more than 33 per cent, profitability will be no worse off than before. If we accept a scenario where sales fall by only 25 per cent as a result of the 10 per cent price increase, we can see that profitability increases by over 100 per cent from £–100 to £+25.

The clear message must be: **do not dismiss the idea of increasing selling prices.**

The price-increase 'ready reckoner' shown below will enable you to evaluate the effect of increasing prices at different margin levels. If our example business increases its selling price by 10 per cent (read along the left-hand scale) for a given gross margin of 20 per cent (read along the top scale), then where these meet (highlighted square) indicates that a 33 per cent reduction in sales volume can occur and the business will be no worse off! In fact if the business loses no more than 33 per cent then it will generate more profit.

Price-increase 'ready reckoner'

		Existing gross margins %								
		5	10	15	20	25	30	35	40	50
	2	29	17	12	9	7	6	5	5	4
%	3	37	23	17	13	11	9	8	7	6
Price	4	44	29	21	17	14	12	10	9	7
increase	5	50	33	25	20	17	14	12	11	9
	7.5	60	43	33	27	23	20	18	16	13
	10	67	50	40	33	29	25	22	20	17
	15	75	60	50	43	37	33	30	27	23

% Volume decrease in sales 'to stand still'

What are the dangers of increasing selling prices?

There is a real chance that if an enterprise increases selling prices it will lose some marginal business – those who rate price as more important than service, quality and availability. A business should therefore think very carefully before putting up prices if:

- It has very few customers – losing one or two could lead to a large reduction in sales revenues and hence profits.
- It has very visible competition – e.g., if one of the high street banks were to introduce bank charges for personal banking then all those customers affected would soon move to other banks that offered free banking.

To counter these effects a business could consider selective and variable price increases. It should evaluate how sensitive each customer (or group of customers) is to price increases and uplift accordingly.

Where can I get further help?

You should look at the following:

- Read *The Genghis Khan Guide to Business* by Brian Warnes (Osmosis Publications, 1987).
- 'I have heard that knowing my break-even point is important – why?' (FAQ 10)

'I've slashed my selling price and am selling more but I am still not making any profit – why?' (FAQ 12)

 ## FAQ 14

'I don't have an accounting system so how can I produce a monthly profit statement quickly and cheaply?'

What do I need to understand first?

If a business knows its break-even point then it knows that any sales above this are contributing extra profit. In fact all those extra sales above the break-even point (BEP) create extra gross margin that automatically becomes net profit. You may have heard the saying that once a business hits BEP all the additional gross margin generated falls straight to the bottom line as net profit. On the other hand if a business is trading below its BEP then the gap between actual sales and break-even sales is contributing loss. Using this principle, a business can generate a 'quick' profit report by knowing (or estimating) just three key figures – sales, gross margin and fixed costs.

How do I use the 'quick' profit report?

The example business we will use has minimal information and is not untypical of many small businesses. Each month it knows what it has sold, usually within a day or two of the month end. At the same time it probably has a pretty good idea of what percentage margin it makes on its sales. It may not know the exact gross margin percentage for that month but it will know what margin it made in an earlier period.

The final figure that it will need to know is the fixed costs for that period. This is quite a straightforward figure to calculate and does not usually change too much from month to month. It is in effect all the business costs that are not already accounted for in the gross margin figure (rent, rates, insurance, office costs, administration salaries, heat, light, finance costs, depreciation, advertising and marketing costs etc.).

Armed with the three key figures – sales, gross margin percentage, and fixed costs – it can produce the 'quick' profit report shown below. The only calculations you need to do are as follows:

Break-even point (see (4) below): This is just the normal BEP calculation of $\dfrac{\text{fixed costs}}{\text{gross margin \%}}$

Break-even gap (see (5) below): This is the key figure because it measures the gap above sales (which represents profitable business) and the gap below (which represents loss generating business).

Quick profit/loss (see (6) below): This takes the gap figure just calculated and measures the profit or loss that this has generated by multiplying it by the gross margin percentage.

Margin of safety (see (7) below): While not required to calculate the 'quick' profit, it shows how vulnerable the business may be to a fall in sales. It shows what percentage sales drop the business could suffer before it became lossmaking. Do note that, if the 'quick' profit shows a loss, then this figure will show what percentage sales increase is needed to achieve break-even sales.

Using the 'quick' profit report

			Month 1
(1)	Sales	£	10,000
(2)	Gross margin %	%	20%
(3)	Fixed costs	£	1,000
(4)	Break-even Point = (3) divided by (2)	£	5,000
(5)	Break-even Gap = (1) less (5)	£	5,000
(6)	Quick profit/loss = (5) times (2)	£	1,000
(7)	Margin of safety = (5) divided by (1) times 100	%	50%

In our example business we can conclude that it has made a profit of £1,000 during the month and that it could sustain a drop in sales of £5,000 (50 per cent × £10,000) before this is wiped out.

What are the limitations of the 'quick' profit report?

You must remember that it is just a profit estimate and that it may be based on several assumptions. Its accuracy will depend on the validity of the assumptions made on gross margin percentage and fixed costs. If these are based on recent historical information (say a previous month or quarter), then unless any large unforeseen changes have occurred the resulting calculations will be quite accurate. However, for any business that does not have any other monthly profit reporting, this is a lifeline – and far better than just relying on bank statements to run business.

Where can I get further help?

You should look at the following:

> ■ Read *The Genghis Khan Guide to Business* by Brian Warnes (Osmosis Publications, 1987).
>
> ■ 'I have heard that knowing my break-even point is important – why?' (FAQ 10)

You will find in the Appendix a blank 12-month version of the 'quick' profit report, which you can use.

FAQ 15

'If I want to improve profitability and cash flow, what is the quickest way to do it?'

What do I need to know?

You must start from a position of some basic knowledge, otherwise you will waste time making changes that will have no benefit. The starting point is to compare the current business performance with that of earlier periods. The best way of identifying where the problems lie is to use a series of accounting ratios (see FAQs 28 to 33 in the section **Questions on business control**). These will identify where the problems lie – it's those areas where the ratios have got worse over recent months and years. However, in many cases there are traditionally four main areas where profit is lost and cash flow is poor:

> ■ gross margin
> ■ overheads
> ■ debtors
> ■ stock

What changes do I have to make?

As businesses grow or mature it is not uncommon for this to be at the expense of performance. I would hazard a guess that most businesses frequently sacrifice gross margin to grow sales. At the same time, as the business grows, debtor control starts to run down. Also, as part of the drive to grow sales, stock levels increase to ensure that no potential sale is lost because stock is not available. Finally, as sales volumes increase, the business start to get 'fat' and overheads increase – an extra person here, there and everywhere. The resulting financial picture is reduced net profit and increased bank overdraft.

So let's concentrate on the four key areas for instant results:

Improving gross margin

There are two ways to improve gross margin. One is to **increase selling prices** – this has been covered to some extent in FAQ 10. For example, if selling price was, say, £40 per unit with a variable cost of £30, a gross margin of £10 or 25 per cent is made on each unit sold. Increase selling price by 10 per cent to £44 and the gross margin will improve to £14 per unit or 32 per cent – an effective increase in gross margin of 28 per cent.

The other method is to **reduce variable costs** – this should be done either in conjunction with the first method or separately. The most immediate ways to reduce costs are to:

- **Change suppliers/renegotiate supply contracts**: Offer to reduce the number of suppliers and put all your business through them in return for lower unit costs. They each get higher volume and so can afford to take a hit on their selling price to you.

- **Change the product/service specification**: VW/Audi group has made its cars significantly cheaper to produce by simplifying production and using more common parts and assemblies. Can you do this to your product range to save money. Alternatively, does your product use overspecified components, when a lower spec/cheaper alternative is available?

- **Improve buying**: Do you get competitive quotes for everything you buy? If not, how do you know your suppliers are not ripping you off? You may not want to change your suppliers but at least check out their prices against the others whom you do not currently use. A non-supplier will quote silly prices to get your business – use this to get a better price off your current suppliers.

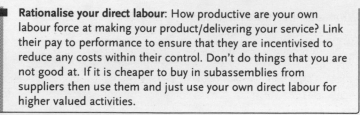

■ **Rationalise your direct labour**: How productive are your own labour force at making your product/delivering your service? Link their pay to performance to ensure that they are incentivised to reduce any costs within their control. Don't do things that you are not good at. If it is cheaper to buy in subassemblies from suppliers then use them and just use your own direct labour for higher valued activities.

Reduce overheads

You can use most of the measures highlighted above to reduce overhead costs. The key thing is to concentrate effort where there is the greatest potential for payback. It's the old 80/20 rule – in this case 80 per cent of the savings can come from 20 per cent of the overhead categories. If your overheads cost £1,000,000 a year do not waste your efforts on some cost category that costs only £5,000 a year (0.5 per cent of the total cost). Look for a category that costs, say, £50,000 a year – a saving of 10 per cent will yield £5,000 (not just £500 as in the other cost category).

Be imaginative. You can cut out a lot of expense before service levels fall – just look at what the banks have done in recent years by getting rid of thousands of employees. IBM made almost every employee justify their existence by reference to the added value they brought in. This helped them get rid of the non-productive administration staff.

Do things differently. A business I knew had several company cars, which covered on average 35,000 business miles each. They had a combination of diesel and petrol vehicles. They decided that by converting all their newer petrol vehicles to LPG they could reduce their fuel costs from around 80p per litre to 40p per litre. Despite the one-off capital cost of around £1,500 per vehicle to convert to LPG, they still made considerable savings. As an added bonus they found that their vehicles were easier to sell as dual-fuel vehicles and were able to recover some of the original conversion cost.

If your interest charges are high and swallowing up most of your profit, then try to renegotiate your borrowings. There are two options:

■ **Rescheduling** – where you extend the term of your existing loans to reduce monthly payments. If things are really tough ask the bank to give you a capital repayment holiday, i.e. an arrangement whereby you pay the interest only for a period of say six to twelve months. This does not improve profitability but it does improve short-term cash flow.

■ **Consolidation** – where you take on one loan to replace all existing loans, usually over a longer period of time but possibly at a lower rate of interest than some of your existing borrowings (e.g., credit cards).

Chase debtors hard

Small businesses do not like chasing money – ask any bank manager and they will confirm this. The problem seems to be that they always see debtors as customers and not as 'villains' who are holding on to cash that should rightfully be yours. To be successful you must depersonalise debt collection. Here are some guidelines that should help get money in faster:

■ **Send out invoices earlier:** You may laugh but if you invoice when the job is done instead of at the end of the month your cash will come in more quickly – especially if your terms are 30 days from date of invoice.

■ **Find out how your customers' payments systems work:** If you supply large businesses you will find that purchase orders are used and that the invoice may have to be sent to head office/purchasing branch first. Also, you will find that there are cut-off days by which invoices have to be authorised for inclusion in that month's payment run. You should also find out about the manual or emergency payments procedure – every business has one – just in case you miss the main run.

■ **Chase overdue payments earlier:** Don't wait until an invoice is overdue before you start chasing. If an invoice is due for payment in, say, five days and that customer has a history of late payment give them a 'courtesy' call to make sure payment will be made on time. This way, if there are any problems (e.g., the invoice has got lost), there is time to get another copy out in time.

■ **Have a system:** It sounds simple but have a system and stick to it. This should include regular debtor review (not just at the month end); follow-up debtor collection procedure (phone call, first letter, legal action); making sure cheques are paid in on day of receipt (not when someone is going into town).

Control stocks

The sole purpose of buying and making stock is to sell it on, as quickly as possible, and for the highest price. On this basis stock holding should be kept to a minimum. It is, however, a balance between having sufficient to meet customer demand and having so much that it becomes obsolete and of no value. Here are some guidelines on how to control stocks.

The first is: link production and stock holding. In too many instances stock is bought almost in 'panic' mode because the business is about to run out or there is no clear idea of how much is needed. To buy the right the amount of stock you need to know the following key information:

- opening stock level: to determine the starting point
- stock reorder time: how quickly can suppliers respond to deliver stock?
- economic reorder quantity: the cheapest (sensible) quantity based on discounts from suppliers and your own costs
- minimum stock-holding level: represents the minimum stock holding you should have based on current sales forecasts and service policy
- next period's production schedule: to determine how much is needed to meet demand

With this information it is then possible to optimise stock buying and minimise stock-holding levels by adopting 'just in time' (JIT) stock holding. This process can be done manually (with difficulty) or with computer software.

The second guideline is: identify slow-moving stocks quickly. The real threat is that you are left with stock that is unusable, owing to obsolescence (e.g., you have stopped making that product so you have no use for a particular stock). The trick is to review stock usage on a regular basis to try to pre-empt this. Computerised stock systems will identify a slowdown in stock usage (e.g., you can view the last 12 months' usage of a stock item). Make sure that those responsible for stock holding are aware of production and marketing requirements.

The third guideline is: liquidate unwanted stock. If you have got stock you can't use then sell it. Don't be hung up on what it cost (that's history): just get some cash in for it. Use the cash to reduce the overdraft or buy the stock you really need.

What will it do for my business?

This will depend on how bad things are to start with and how much effort you put in. However, even a small improvement in all the areas shown above will have a big improvement when consolidated in a business. In the example shown below we can see how even a 5 per cent improvement in these areas has led to a 145 per cent improvement in net profit. It has also led to a significant improvement in working capital, due to reduced debtor and stock funding.

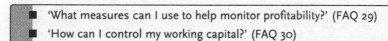

Effect of 5% change on key areas	Before	After
Sales	240,000	252,000
Cost of sales	144,000	136,800
Gross margin	96,000	115,200
Overheads	80,000	76,000
Net profit	16,000	39,200
Debtors	60,000	57,000
Stock	36,000	34,200
Debtors + stock %	40%	36%

Based on this example it must make sense to work on margins, overheads, debtors and stocks.

Where can I get further help?

You should look at the following:

- 'What measures can I use to help monitor profitability?' (FAQ 29)
- 'How can I control my working capital?' (FAQ 30)

FAQ 16

'What is more important, profit or cash?'

What do I need to know?

You need to know where your business is in its life cycle because this will determine whether it should be generating profit or cash, or both.

Stages of business development
The needs of a start-up business and a more mature-growth business are quite different. In simple terms the business life cycle can be shown as follows:

> ■ **Start-up:** During the first couple of years the issues are mostly to do with survival – finding customers (and keeping them), making sure products/services keep up with changing customer needs.
>
> ■ **Early years:** During this period the main issues relate to consolidating the business – controlling the business, staff recruitment and retention, management structure.
>
> ■ **Growth and maturity years:** During the rest of its life it faces the challenges of expansion – securing appropriate funding, moving premises, moving into new markets and new products, competing with bigger businesses, mergers/acquisitions, disposals, protecting its position, making a good return.

If we start to examine the business in each of these stages it will become much clearer what is more important, profit or cash.

Start-up business

It is unrealistic to expect a new business to make profit from day one – even bank managers accept this. It is common practice for most small businesses to be unprofitable for the first three to six months, with the first year being break-even or marginal profit. Larger start-up enterprises, such as the dotcom companies, would not be aiming to break even for several years. So it is clear that for most start-up business profit is not the most important consideration. So what are the priorities?

> ■ **Infrastructure** – getting the people, the marketing, the selling, the product and the production right.
>
> ■ **Milestones** – making sure that objectives are met on schedule (e.g., the product is ready for sale when the business said it would be).
>
> ■ **Achieving volume sales** – making sure that the business is able to sell at the level predicted, whether there will be any slippage.
>
> ■ **Achieving break-even** – ensuring that within a reasonable time the budget can and will achieve break-even.

For the most part all of this activity is set against time scales and cash flow – is it on time and on budget. The conclusion must be that at this stage in a business cash is more important than profit. Since the business is not generating any significant cash flow then the critical areas will be:

- **Initial funding** – ensuring that the business is not underfunded from the outset. One of the major causes of failure among start-up businesses is not having enough cash in the first place to see them through until sustainable profitability. This can be avoided by doing a start-up cash flow forecast (as well as the profit forecast).
- **Access to funds** – ensuring that the business has further cash available as and when it needs it. As you will have learned by now, growing businesses are great consumers of cash so additional ongoing funding will be needed.

Early years

Once the business has made it past start-up the focus changes. Having started to trade profitably the business must develop. It must now seek to grow both sales and profit while ensuring that both are sustainable in the future. At the same time it must start to consolidate its position to ensure that its existence does not come under threat. The business should during this period have achieved reliable profitability and cash flow. The priorities are now:

- **Managing the business** – making sure that a management structure is in place, key staff are tied in and that the business has good financial control and management information. This will be a period of investment in resources.
- **Ensuring repeatability** – making sure that what you have done to get to this stage can be repeated (e.g., new products can and are being developed; production is optimised and improved; new customers are being developed).

For the most part all this activity is set against improving profit – cash flow is a secondary consideration. Most businesses at this stage should be capable of generating their own cash flow sufficient for survival. The critical areas will be:

- **Growth** – making sure that growth does not prejudice profitability. It is a well-known fact that in many cases as sales grow profitability does not grow at the same rate.
- **Security** – making sure that the business is not placed at risk as a result of it trading (e.g., bad debts, overtrading, claims from customers for faulty products/services).

Growth and maturity years

By now the business has achieved long-term survival – it is profitable and capable of good cash flow generation. Any additional funding requirement will be for specific projects that are large-scale and to lift the business up to a higher plane. This may include projects such as moving to larger premises to accommodate increased sales. It is likely to include other organic activities, such as buying up competitors or selling off non-core business activities. The priorities are now:

- **Expansion** – looking for ways to change the business by taking it to a higher level. This will include product and market diversification brought about by lack of growth potential in existing markets with existing products. It could also include striking strategic alliances with other parties to move the business forward.

- **Strategic** – planning the end game for the business. This could involve a trade sale (for an existing owner-manager) or a flotation (for a business committed to accelerated growth).

At this stage the business should be highly profitable and looking for new ways to grow profitably. Cash flow should no longer be an issue – it has sufficient cash to fund all day-to-day activities. However, mega-expansion will require outside funding support. The critical areas will be:

- **Protecting its position** – the enterprise is now very conscious of the changing outside world and the impact that it may have on its business. The main activity is to protect the business, which is usually done by size and diversity. It is a recognised fact that larger businesses are less susceptible to failure. At the same time the business should be constantly monitoring and trying to improve all aspects of business performance – margins, debtor collection. Stock management etc.

- **Exit route** – at this stage it is decision time for many owner-managers. If they are still young then the plan may be to continue to grow the business. However, for many this may be the time to groom their business for disposal (see FAQs 19 and 20).

Overall conclusion – profit or cash?

It is clear that it depends on the stage of development of the business. However, there is a saying that in the short term all businesses need cash but in the long term profit is vital. Basically this means that in the short term unprofitable businesses can survive by 'massaging' their cash flow. They do this by delaying payments; getting customers to pay up front in exchange for cash discounts; selling off assets. While they can do this for a few months it is not sustainable because without profit no new wealth is created and so all the asset base will eventually disappear.

Where can I get further help?

You should look at the following:

> ■ Read *The Genghis Khan Guide to Business* by Brian Warnes (Osmosis Publications, 1987).
>
> ■ 'If I want to improve profitability and cash flow, what is the quickest way to do it?' (FAQ 15)

CHAPTER THREE

Questions on longer-term funding

FAQ 17

'What is a business angel and where can I find one?'

What do I need to know?

Business angels are usually high-worth individuals who make equity (shares purchase) investments in businesses. Quite frequently, as well as money, they can bring valuable skills and contacts to a business. They will typically commit amounts of between £10,000 and £100,000 to a single business. Where a larger sum is required they will often work in a syndicate with others. Business angels are usually serial investors and will make more than one investment each year and over several years. They will invest in businesses at any stage of their life but tend to support at an early stage – start-up or early expansion. They are catholic in their tastes: they will invest in most business sectors. They are, however, quite parochial and will usually invest in businesses close to where they live or work.

How do they operate?

They operate quite informally either on their own or through business-angel networks. In most respects they operate in the same way as venture-capital firms – investments are made primarily for financial gain. However, quite frequently they will have more than one reason for investing in a business, which may well work to the advantage of the business receiving the investment. They may want to play an active role (part time) in the business in which they are investing. This gives them the chance to use their business skills for the benefit of both parties. A further benefit is that as business people they may be able to bring useful contacts that the business can benefit from.

The key factors they take into account are those that any venture capitalist would regard as important. In addition, there are other considerations that are specific to business angels.

- They may be prepared to accept lower returns than a venture capitalist if there is the opportunity to be involved.
- They will always be minority shareholders, so they are not a threat to current control of the business.
- They are likely to be able to make quick investment decisions (quicker than a venture capitalist), which will save time and money during the process.
- They are prepared to make longer-term investments but will seek similar exit routes to a venture capitalist.
- They are unlikely to make more than one investment in a business, owing to their more limited funds.

Where can I find one?

Unfortunately, business angels want to remain anonymous so you will not find them in the Yellow Pages – this stops them from being swamped with proposals. It also means that they can be found only through business-angel networks, which act as introduction services. Fortunately, these business networks are quite visible and there are over forty listed in the British Venture Capital Association's *Sources of Business Angel Capital*, which gives a profile of each together with contact details.

You will find that your local Business Link is also a good starting point to contact business angels. They will often arrange 'beauty parades', whereby businesses wanting funding have a chance to present their business proposition to a panel of business angels.

Where can I get further help?

You should look at the following:

> ■ The British Venture Capital Association (BVCA), *Sources of Business Angel Capital* publication (published annually) BVCA, Essex House, 12–13 Essex Street, London WC2 3AA.
>
> ■ Contact your local Business Link.

FAQ 18

'I have got a great business idea but it's a bit risky – who should I go to for money?'

What do I need to know?

Unfortunately you have probably found out that banks do not like to fund propositions with a strong element of business risk. Because they can only lend money (they can't do equity deals), they are paranoid about losing it if the business goes bust. Consequently, most bank managers are unable to fund a business that does not have sufficient assets to act as security for the loan. They also want to deal with established businesses. In effect, this means that banks seek to eliminate all risk.

However, there are organisations that specialise in funding business propositions that have risk. These are venture capitalists and over the last thirty years they have become the main source of risk capital in the UK. Their primary means of supporting businesses is through the provision of equity funding: they buy shares in the company they are supporting. Equity funding is acknowledged as the correct method of risk funding as shown in the funding matrix below.

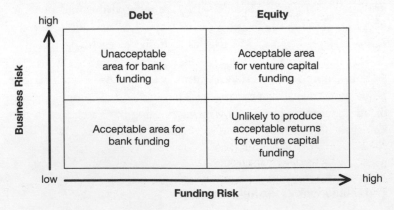

How does venture capital work?

The important thing to recognise is that equity funding is quite different from bank funding. Banks make loans and are repaid capital and interest according to an agreed schedule. They can lend to any type of business organisation – sole trader, partnerships, limited companies. Venture capitalists give money to a business in exchange for pieces of paper, called share certificates. They are buying a share of the company and as such do not have such a clearly defined route for the return of their money. Their expectation is that at some time in the future the business will pay dividends and that their investment will grow in value. They will get their money back only when someone else buys either their shares or the whole company's shares. Equity funding is available only to limited companies.

The starting point is to find a venture-capital provider and to do this you will need a business plan. This will detail your business proposition, the funding you require, how and when it is required, financial projections and details of the business's performance to date. To help you find the right venture-capital provider you will need to be specific about one or two things.

Stage of funding

Venture-capital providers do not fund every stage of business development and each has its own preferences. The recognised stages for funding are.

- Start-up: Financing for product development and early marketing. At this stage the product has not been sold commercially.

- Other early stage: Financing for commercial manufacturing and sales. At this stage the company will not have generated any profit.

- Expansion financing: As its name implies this is financing to increase production, marketing, product development, additional working capital for established businesses. Can also include recovery funding and refinancing of bank debt.

- Secondary purchase: Buying existing shares from another venture-capital provider or other shareholders.

- Management buy-out (MBO): Funding the purchase of a company by the current management team.

- Management buy-in (MBI): Funding the purchase of a company by an outside management team.

> ■ Institutional buy-out (IBO): Funding the purchase of a company by a venture-capital provider prior to the management team (either existing or new) acquiring a stake in the company.
>
> ■ Leveraged build-up (LBU): Where a venture-capital provider buys a company with the purpose of making further acquisitions to create a larger business group.

Industry sector

By the same reasoning each venture-capital provider has its own sector preferences and will generally not make investments outside these. The common sector descriptions are: Agriculture, Biotechnology, Chemical & material, Communications, Computer-related, Consumer-related, Construction & property, Energy, Environmental, Financial services, Food, Industrial automation, Industrial products & services, Leisure, Media, Medical/health-related, Other electronics related, Other manufacturing, Retail, Transportation, Investment outside UK.

After you have identified and approached an appropriate venture-capital provider who will be interested in your industry sector and stage of funding, the next stage is to negotiate and conclude the deal. While this is a simplification of a process that will involve lawyers, accountants and considerable time and money, it is essentially the rest of the process (it is covered in more detail in FAQ 19). However, at the end of this process you will have agreed:

> ■ a valuation for your business
> ■ the amount of funding you will receive
> ■ what share of your business the venture capitalist will acquire in return for their money
> ■ the terms of the deal (contract) incorporating how the business will be managed and controlled
> ■ an outline exit route and time scale

Where do I find one?

Fortunately, it is considerably easier to find a venture-capital provider than a business angel since they are actively looking for business proposals. All the reputable venture-capital providers belong to the British Venture Capital Association (BVCA), who provide a directory of UK-based venture-capital providers. This has a profile on each one covering such details as:

- address, telephone number, email and website address
- size – people and money invested
- where they get their money from
- how many companies they have invested in
- minimum and maximum investment amounts
- stage and industry preferences
- geographical preferences
- whom to contact

However, before you make any formal approach it is recommended that you talk with your financial adviser and make sure your business plan is up to scratch.

Where can I get further help?

You should look at the following:

- The British Venture Capital Association (BVCA) Directory (published annually). BVCA, Essex House, 12–13 Essex Street, London WC2 3AA.
- Read *The Best-Laid Business Plans* by Paul Barrow (Virgin Publishing, 2001).
- 'I have heard that Venture Capital is a rip-off – how do I make sure I don't get done?' (FAQ 19)

FAQ 19

'I have heard that venture capital is a rip-off – how do I make sure I don't get done?'

What do I need to know?

In FAQ 18 we skirted over the finer detail of how to negotiate an equity deal with a venture capitalist. However, it is like any other deal: everything is negotiable. The problem is that most people do this kind of deal only a handful of times in their lives, whereas venture capitalists do it day in and day out. No wonder they have earned themselves the 'vulture capitalist' tag. However, all you need to remember are the following principles:

> ■ The deal is made up many elements, of which price (how much your business is worth) is just one (e.g., management package, day-to-day control, non-executive directors, reporting, etc.). There is flexibility in all of these areas.
>
> ■ A deal is a good deal only if both sides are fully on board. If one party feels 'screwed', especially the management, they do not feel motivated. If they are not motivated they will not deliver maximum performance for the business and the value of the business will not be maximised.
>
> ■ Don't go into the 'bear pit' alone. If you are trying to raise, say, a £2 million equity deal then take it very seriously and make sure you are represented by the best lawyer and accountant available. The difference between a good team and a bad team of advisers may only be £10,000–20,000 in cost. In the scheme of things this is hardly worth considering – they will pay for themselves in the help they give.

Finally, remember that the quality and strength of your business plan is key to getting a good deal. If it shows your business proposition in a good light then half the work is already done. If it is poor and full of holes and mistakes then you will have an uphill struggle to get any deal at all.

Negotiating and completing the deal

Let me tell you now that deals are not done overnight and the more you want, the longer it can take and the more it will cost you. For example, if you wanted £100,000 then this would be within the scope of a business angel to provide. This is a fairly informal process and does not need a lawyer. If the investment was being provided by a single investor, a good accountant could do the whole process within a few hours of his time and within, say, a month of elapsed time. The arrangement costs could be a few hundred pounds.

On the other hand if you were raising, say, £1 million via a venture-capital provider the process is both longer and more expensive. Lawyers and accountants will be involved on both sides. A progress called 'due diligence' will be gone through – this is where the team putting forward the business plan guarantee that they are not telling porkies. Such a deal might take three months to complete and have costs of £50,000 for the various advisers and so forth.

Please always remember that everything is negotiable (it does bear repeating) and, if you feel strongly about something, stick to your guns. If you are raising a large sum of money via venture capital there will be a subscription agreement or similar lengthy legal tome. This lays out the rules of the game. It will include a number of things, like these set out below.

What package you and your senior management team can have
This means salary, cars, pension, other perks, service contracts, tie-ins etc. Don't short-change yourself. If you are currently underpaid don't spend the next few years like this – it does not suit an investor to have you demotivated. Stick out for what you believe is right. Also, don't forget that the deal you sign up to may be for five years, so make sure that you factor in good increases.

How you can run the business
This means what authorisation is required and when. For example, a venture capitalist will attempt to restrict your ability to spend money without their authority (e.g., capital projects above £5,000 may need authority; unplanned revenue items above £1,000 may also need authority). If these will effectively tie your hands and stop you from managing the business, tell them and get reasonable limits set. They don't know what is realistic and sensible for your business – so they will have to listen to you.

Day-to-day running of the business
The key figures from your business plan will be embodied in the agreement – in effect, you are contracting to deliver those profit figures. If you go according to plan, all will be sweetness and light. If you do not, all manner of nasty penalties may descend on you. Read carefully what these may be and do not agree with them if they seem unfair. For example, the venture capitalist may claim that a failure to deliver the agreed level sales points to poor sales direction and management. Using this excuse, they may want to force you to appoint a very expensive sales director, which they will claim is their right under the subscription agreement. Don't give them the right to make senior appointments.

Non-executive directors and reporting

This is the venture capitalist's way of interfering in/influencing your business. You must of course understand their position. If they have just given you £1 million they don't want to lose it, so they want to take out a little extra insurance. It may be that a non-executive finance director is a great idea – in that case grab him/her with both arms if it does not cost too much. If the non-executive is going to cost a lot you should question the value for money – how much and how many days a month do you get? If they want quarterly accounts then I would say that is reasonable. If they want monthly accounts, question why, and kick if you don't like it.

The ratchet

This is the way venture capitalists like to incentivise senior managers in the business. Basically, it is a way of giving you more shares for above-business-plan performance. The rationale is quite straightforward. If you can make the business more profitable it will be worth more when it comes to disposing of it. If you can do that you will make them richer so they are prepared to give a bit of this extra profit back to you – not as cash but as shares. You can negotiate the detail of the ratchet.

The factors affecting the price (valuation of your business)

There are five main factors that affect the valuation and all these are open to negotiation (to some extent):

- the perceived risk in your business
- your customer base
- maintainable profits
- required rate of return
- industry price/earnings (P/E) ratio

To the inexperienced outsider these may seem like fact, but they are all open to interpretation. For example, you may consider that there is little scope for interpreting maintainable profit. It is of course based on the figures that you put forward in your business plan. However, this will include the 'extortionate' package that you and your fellow directors are taking as owner managers – salaries (yours and your wife's/husband's/partner's), pension, cars, dividends etc. My suggestion is that when it comes to evaluating maintainable profits you should argue that all these should be added back to the business profits and replaced by a more modest level as if the business were being run by salaried managers. This is common practice.

What do I do next?

It depends on what stage you are at and how much money you are trying to raise. If you have already started negotiations then you must take a view as to what sort of deal you believe you have and how desperate you are for the money now. It may be that you need the money now and that there is no merit in stopping or renegotiating now. If you are just starting out, then get the best help at a cost commensurate with the amount of money being raised. For example, if you are raising £50,000–100,000 on a business angel type of deal, then use your own accountants (assuming they are chartered accountants). They can do the whole deal. If you are raising big money – £300,000 upwards – then use the local office of a Top 10 UK firm of chartered accountants and follow their advice.

Where can I get further help?

You should look at the following:

- The British Venture Capital Association (BVCA) Directory (published annually). BVCA, Essex House, 12–13 Essex Street, London WC2 3AA.
- Read *The Best-Laid Business Plans* by Paul Barrow (Virgin Publishing, 2001).
- Contact your accountant or financial adviser.

FAQ 20

'I am thinking of selling my business – how do I value it?'

What do I need to know?

Let me say something up front. While valuing a business is a well-trodden process, there will be times when a business will be worth more (or less) than the underlying financial projections. This may be due to the venture capitalist or business angel wanting to do the deal with you because they want your type of business in their portfolio.

On the other hand, if they have already invested in too many businesses like yours (sector/size) that year, they will try to give you such a rotten deal as to drive you away. Also, do make sure that you are prepared to stand up for yourself and don't forget to look at FAQ 19 for help on this.

Of course, I can't give away all my valuation secrets – otherwise I will get thrown out of the magic circle. However, I can tell you the basic rules, which are incredibly simple.

How will they value your business?

Assuming that the investor is interested in your business then the following are the key factors taken into account in valuing a business:

The perceived risk

If this is a new business with no track record, unproven management and a new product/service, then this will attract a high-risk rating. On the other hand, if the business and management have a track record and the product/service is already recognised (it is just doing it quicker/better/cheaper/faster), then this will be seen as having very little risk. This factor may be used to adjust the required rate of return or downgrade the future value of the business.

Your customer base

If the business plan shows a good spread of customers with none accounting for, say, more than 10 per cent of your sales, then this will be favoured. On the other hand, if the business has a small customer base it will be seen as very vulnerable and this will concern an investor. This factor may be used to adjust the required rate of return or downgrade the future value of the business.

Maintainable profits

This is key to the valuation of a business. An investor will value a business on what he believes its future maintainable post-tax profits will be. Of course, it is quite likely that the Year 3 profits are projected to be higher than Year 1 – that's OK but an investor will discount profit forecasts further than one year ahead, so it may not be advantageous to base a valuation on, say Year 3 profit forecasts.

Required rate of return

This will obviously affect valuation. Let's say that a risk-free investment (e.g., building society) is yielding 5 per cent. An investor may want 20 per cent per year, which equates to a return of 2.5 times their original investment over five years, for a low-risk investment (as measured by the first three categories above). On the other hand, this same investor may want 40 per cent per year, which equates to a return of 5.4 times their original investment over five years, for a higher-risk investment. You may think this is greedy but if they make higher-risk investments then the chances are that out of, say, every ten investments six will go bust – so the remaining four have to make a higher return to achieve an acceptable result overall.

Industry price/earnings (P/E) ratio

The final consideration must be how many years' worth of profits is the investor paying for to arrive at the future value for the business. If you have, say, an engineering business making £50,000 per annum (and capable of making it for many more years), would you be prepared to sell it for £50,000 (one year's worth of earnings)? Of course not. So how many years' worth of profits should an investor pay for?

For more traditional business where maximum profitability is being achieved now (such as engineering), the P/E ratio (or profit multiple) is likely to be low – say three to six times. That means that an investor will pay three to six times the annual maintainable profits to arrive at the future value of this business.

On the other hand, where the business is in a new and innovative sector (the Internet-based businesses are a good example of this) where maximum profitability is not being achieved, the P/E ratio may be as high as 20 or 30 times – because the investor is expecting better to come.

The choice of P/E ratio will have a profound effect on the future value of the business. It is not enough to look in the *Financial Times* and take an average P/E from there because these businesses are quoted (therefore have a larger market for the shares) and bigger (therefore a lower risk). The correct approach is to look for similar businesses that have sold recently – this may come from talking to an experienced intermediary – and adopting a similar P/E.

The final part of the equation, which does not affect the valuation, but does affect how much equity an investor will receive, is the amount of money you need. For example, if a business is valued at £150,000 and the owners want to raise £50,000, an investor will get 33.33 per cent of the equity (50,000/150,000).

An example with some numbers

OK, let's look at an example to see how it could all work out in practice. Beechwood Enterprises Limited has been trading for one year as metal finishers with an inexperienced management team. To fund its next stage of growth it has decided to raise £150,000 by means of an equity investment. Its projections are as shown below:

	Turnover	Profit after tax
Current year	£375,000	£37,500
Year 1	£500,000	£62,500
Year 2	£662,000	£75,000
Year 3	£850,000	£112,500

Let's assume that a P/E ratio of six times has been agreed and that the investor is looking for a 35 per cent return because they perceive the business to be high-risk. How, then, should we value this business?

Stage 1: What is the future value (FV) of the business?

Using the formula: FV = maintainable profits × P/E value

Year 1 Profit £62,500 × 6 (P/E) = £375,000 future value
Year 2 Profit £75,000 × 6 (P/E) = £450,000 future value
Year 3 Profit £112,500 × 6 (P/E) = £675,000 future value

On the face of things it looks straightforward – we should choose the year that yields the highest value, which is Year 3 profits. Well, because this is two years away, our investor will discount this by 35 per cent for each year away. So let's look at these three years again applying this factor and using the following formula:

$$\text{Present value (PV)} = \frac{\text{Future value (FV)}}{(1 + i)^n}$$

Where : i = Investor's required rate of return
         n = Number of years until forecast profits

$$\text{Year 1: PV} = \frac{375,000}{(1 + 0.35)^1} = \frac{375,000}{1.35} = £277,777$$

$$\text{Year 2: PV} = \frac{450,000}{(1 + 0.35)^2} = \frac{450,000}{1.8225} = £246,913$$

$$\text{Year 3: PV} = \frac{675,000}{(1 + 0.35)^3} = \frac{675,000}{2.460375} = £274,348$$

On this basis it clearly makes sense to use Year 1 forecast profits because this yields a present value of £277,777. The other years yield lower present value because of the discount factor being used.

Stage 2: How much equity will the investor acquire?

The final stage is quite straightforward and calculates how much equity they will get for their £150,000. Having established that the business is worth £277,777 then £150,000 buys 150,000/277,777 = 54 per cent of the equity.

Where can I get further help?

You should look at the following:

- The British Venture Capital Association (BVCA) Directory (published annually). BVCA, Essex House, 12–13 Essex Street, London WC2 3AA.
- Read *The Best-Laid Business Plans* by Paul Barrow (Virgin Publishing, 2001).
- Institute of Chartered Accountants in England and Wales, PO Box 433, Chartered Accountants Hall, Moorgate Place, London EC2P 2BJ (020 7920 8100).

FAQ 21

'How do I get the best price for my business when I sell it?'

What do I need to know?

As you can see, the calculation is quite simple (see FAQ 19), except that the five key factors used to calculate the value can lead to a whole range of different valuations, even though the formula used is the same. Small variances in any of these can lead to a huge difference in valuation. However, there are a whole range of 'confidence' factors that can make or break a deal. If you are planning to sell your business then you should 'groom' it for disposal. This may mean that you go through a 'window-dressing' process that may take two to three years to make your business look as attractive as possible to a potential buyer. You will make short-term decisions, which, while not to the detriment of the long-term health of the business, are definitely geared towards selling up for the best possible price.

The following are the main areas to focus your attention on to ensure you sell your business for the best possible price.

Improve earnings by improving sales and cutting costs

A business is bought primarily for its maintainable profit stream. However, you need to think more imaginatively about profit creation than before. The first step has got to be to hike up the sales as quickly as possible. You will find that there is usually a minimum turnover level needed to attract a buyer. This will of course vary from sector to sector, but £5–10 million is often quoted. If your business is currently turning over £2 million and £5 million is the required level, then your 'grooming' period could well be three or more years, during which you speed up sales growth to this target.

Maximising profitability means taking short-term actions that yield a big payback. Look at your maintenance budget to see what is discretionary and can be cut out. If the plan is to repaint premises every three years and they are looking OK, don't spend the money. Look at the head count and make sure there is no overstaffing. Need to save more cost? Renegotiate all your key supplies. If there is a choice between a revenue alternative and a capital alternative then choose the capital spend. Why? Revenue spend is 100 per cent against profit whereas capital is depreciated, which may mean a hit of only 25 per cent or something similar against profits.

Make sure that a capable management team is in place

Make sure the business can survive without you. This means ensuring there is an effective management team in place. This costs money and takes time, so start now. The payback is a more saleable business. Businesses that are still dependent on the owner-manager are virtually unsaleable. Ask yourself the question, 'What would happen to my business if I could not work for three months?' A friend of mine suffered a heart attack and could not work for three months. Much to his amazement (and relief) his staff rose to the challenge and the business thrived. He got better and decided to sell the business. Within two years he had done just that, and now lives abroad as a tax exile.

Target one or more potential buyers

Common sense says that you need to court more than one potential suitor to get some sort of 'bidding competition'. Start to think early on about who might want your business and their reasons. Do you have a bigger competitor to whom you are a pain in the neck? Do you have a major customer who might like to buy you to safeguard supplies? Are you so profitable that a larger predator might want you as part of a diversification plan?

This should give you a short list of potential buyers. Do your homework on them – get their accounts, start to talk with them, develop a close relationship with their senior managers, generally get close to them so they know you and you know them. The objective of this activity is to make sure that the grapevine is working on your behalf and that they are already thinking about how your business would fit in with theirs.

Trade buyers pay more than venture capitalists

A trade buyer will see more in your business than any venture capitalist. I have known unprofitable businesses to sell for a large premium to a trade buyer because they knew that they could make it profitable by integrating it into their business (cost savings). Also, it could enable a trade buyer to open out your customer base and secure a greater degree of market dominance.

There are so many more reasons for a trade buyer to pay a good price, because they will understand your business. They will also tend to be far more generous in the price earnings multiple that they apply to the valuation (see FAQ 19).

Another good reason for selling to a trade buyer is speed and cost. They tend to move faster than venture capitalists because fewer people are involved. If the board of a competitor decide to buy your business it will happen in weeks and you will deal with probably just their solicitor. Also, since they already understand your business and the marketplace, they don't need to bring in other consultants or advisers. Venture capitalists will not have the same level of knowledge and will need accountants, solicitors, product specialists, market specialists and so forth to make sure they get it right. This means meetings will be time-consuming and very expensive.

Be ready when a buyer makes a move

Part of the process of buying/selling a business is something called 'due diligence'. This process involves the buyer in investigating all manner of things such as liabilities for claims for faulty products, ownership of brands, trade marks, patents and other property. If you can pre-empt their questions and have the answers and evidence available, you will speed up the process. In addition, your buyer will ask you to 'warrant' any statements that you have made. In effect they will ask you to provide the proof that any statements you have made are true and that you will be liable if they turn out to be untrue later. The likely comeback will be that the selling price will be retrospectively reduced.

Don't say yes to the first offer that comes along

After all the hard work you have done in getting your business ready for sale, it must be very gratifying to receive an offer. However, the chances are that this offer is just exploratory – just checking to see if you will be insulted by their derisory offer. Treat this process a bit like negotiating in an Eastern bazaar for some trinket and you will not go far wrong. Remember there are three golden rules:

> ■ They have a maximum price that they are prepared to pay for your business based on sound financial analysis – but will always offer lower than this to start off with.
>
> ■ You should have an absolute minimum price that you will not go below – be prepared to tell the buyer this and why this price is the bottom line.
>
> ■ You have only one business to sell (usually), so you do not have another chance to make up for any lost financial benefit.

Do not get obsessed with price and think more about the benefit to you. For example, if you have decided that you need £3 million for your business, so you can retire in comfort, then your financial objective is to retire in comfort. It is highly likely that a deal can be structured that more than meets this objective but effectively values your business at £2.5 million. The structure of this deal may involve loan notes (to avoid capital gains tax), share options (if buyer is a quoted company), pension contributions etc. So remember the end objective and make sure you receive it.

You may be interested to know that a friend of mine was approached by a small, fast-growing, publicly quoted medical group with a view to buying his business. We went to meet the prospective buyer and listened to their offer and what they had to say about their prospects for the future. The offer amounted to about £2 million, of which 30 per cent would be cash and the rest shares. We departed and after some deliberation we took the view that we felt that they needed my friend's company more than he needed their money. Within two months the offer had risen to £4 million, of which 50 per cent would be cash, with a ratchet taking the valuation up to £6 million. Now the deal was starting to look good.

Let capable advisers manage the selling process

Selling a business takes on average three to six months and is something way beyond the capability of most owner-managers. There are two main issues to consider during the process of selling a business:

> - the legal process of structuring and completing the deal
> - the continuing need to run the business while the sale is negotiated and completed

Fortunately, if you are selling to a trade buyer the process is simplified and has a shorter time scale. However, my own experience as a venture capitalist is that during the period that the deal is being negotiated and completed most owner-managers take their eye off the ball and their businesses start to decline. The constant meetings, phone calls, requests for information etc. are both tiring and a distraction from the day-to-day running of the business. The reality is that you need two teams – one to run the business and one to run the deal. Let the lawyers and accountant do the deal work – brief them and leave them to it. You make sure that the business continues to thrive in the meantime.

Where can I get further help?

You should look at the following:

> - The British Venture Capital Association (BVCA) Directory (published annually). BVCA, Essex House, 12–13 Essex Street, London WC2 3AA.
> - Read *The Best-Laid Business Plans* by Paul Barrow (Virgin Publishing, 2001).
> - Institute of Chartered Accountants in England and Wales, PO Box 433, Chartered Accountants Hall, Moorgate Place, London EC2P 2BJ (020 7920 8100).

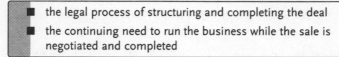

FAQ 22

'If I take on an equity partner, how can I be sure they won't take over my business, and how do I get rid of them?'

What do I need to know?

You should regard taking on venture capital just like a modern wedding, except that divorce is openly discussed at the start as part of the prenuptial contract. When a business takes on a venture-capital partner then several issues are discussed and agreed right from the start:

- the initial split in ownership of the equity of the business
- the mechanism for 'giving' equity to management (ratchet)
- day-to day-control
- exit strategy

The objective is to make sure that these work to the benefit of both parties – get these right at the start and there will not be a problem. It is also worthwhile remembering that each party to the deal has their own skills and responsibilities. No one knows a business better than its management. Believe it or not, that is also what venture capitalists think, and that is why they want the management to run the business. Venture capitalists have usually never run a business before, so they have very limited business experience.

The other vital factor is to consider right from the start the likely exit route and timing, so that both sides (management and venture capitalist) can be working towards this common goal.

Control and ownership of the business

Some years ago I was a director of a venture-capital provider when we were approached by a business that needed to raise about £750,000 on a business valued at £850,000. When we did the initial calculation it showed that we would have to acquire something like 90 per cent of the equity. Neither party really wanted this because we believed that the management would feel that we owned the business. We had every confidence in the management team and we wanted to ensure that they had a significant share of the equity. Usually, when an equity deal is done, the venture-capital provider wants to take on about 15–30 per cent of the equity. This way it ensures that the existing management remain in control and there is still scope for additional funding should more finance be needed.

So how did we do a deal that ensured that both parties were happy? We decided to structure a package that improved the management position both at the start and in three years' time. It was believed that the management needed a deal that let them retain about 30 per cent of the equity now, with the ability to bring this up to 50 per cent later. We were also agreed that there was no way that we could increase the valuation of the business at the start to artificially give the management extra equity. The key elements of the deal were as follows:

1. Initial funding deal

Rather than give the business £750,000 in a straight equity deal, a 'mixed' deal was arranged aimed at ensuring a more acceptable 70/30 per cent mix. This was done as shown in the table below.

Mixed-funding deal to provide £750,000 for business worth £850,000					
		Original		Final	
Ordinary shares		750,000	88%	575,000	68%
Redeemable preference shares	9%/3 years	0		100,000	
Third-party soft loan		0		75,000	
Total funding		750,000		750,000	

Key to making this work was to switch some £175,000 from ordinary shares to some other form of funding. This was done by arranging a third-party loan of £75,000 – a brewery provided this against future beer sales. A further £100,000 of redeemable preference shares were issued with a ticket (interest rate) of 9 per cent and redeemable in full in three years' time. While these were technically shares, they were in effect a loan, carrying an interest rate of 9 per cent and repayable in three years' time. They carried no voting rights, so did not count for control purposes.

Based on this mixed package we acquired 68 per cent of the equity, leaving the existing management with 32 per cent.

By using a little imagination we were able to do a deal that met the initial objective of leaving the management with a reasonable level of ownership. How, then, did we give them the future hope of boosting their share of the ownership to 50 per cent later? This was done using a ratchet.

2. Ratchet

The purpose of the ratchet is to make sure the management really deliver maximum profit from the business because this is the major factor in valuing it. In the business plan the valuation of the business was based on net profit of £141,750 per annum at a P/E of 6 in Year 3. It was agreed that, if net profit fell within the range of 15 per cent to 55 per cent above the base figure (£141,750 per annum) in Year 3, then the management would see their ownership of the equity increase from 32 per cent to 50 per cent. The effect of the ratchet is shown in the table below.

Ratchet

	Year 3	Ratchet options ---------->				
	Original	1	2	3	4	5
		15%	20%	25%	30%	55%
Net profit	141,750	163,013	170,100	177,188	184,275	219,713
P/E	6	6	6	6	6	6
Value	850,500	978,075	1,020,600	1,063,125	1,105,650	1,318,275
Equity split:						
VC	68%	63%	62%	60%	58%	50%
Management	32%	37%	38%	40%	42%	50%

As a safety precaution we installed a safety net to protect us (the venture capitalist). Should net profit slip back by more than 5 per cent in the two years following the third year, then the ratchet would be recalculated (downwards). This ensured that the management team did not ease off after earning their extra equity.

I am sure that the more observant of you may have spotted an apparent mistake (especially if you have read FAQ 19) in the valuation of a business at £850,000 based on profits in three years' time without applying a discount factor. We did apply a discount factor but for the sake of simplicity I have used unadjusted figures in this example.

This was a self-funding arrangement because, even as the venture capitalist (VC) share fell from 68 per cent to 50 per cent, their investment grew in value by 14 per cent. At the same time the management saw an even greater return for their efforts (see table below).

	68%	50%	Increase
VC	578,340	659,138	14%
Management	272,160	659,138	142%

As you can see in this example, the sharing of equity for above planned growth seems to offer a virtuous circle – management have the incentive to work harder and obtain the majority of the extra benefit without its disadvantaging the venture capitalist.

3. Day-to-day control

This has already been touched on in FAQ 19. The whole area of day-to-day reporting and control is negotiated at the start and then included in the subscription agreement (contract). On the basis that the venture capitalist and the management have agreed a level of profit performance over the next 3–5 years, then there is in effect a contract to deliver this. However, the management team must be given enough flexibility to run the business in such a way that they *can* deliver. This is why the management are in a very strong position to argue that they need a high level of freedom to make decisions and run the business with the minimum of red tape and interference.

The problem arises when the business does not deliver net profits at the level set out in the business plan. The venture capitalist feels the need to become more 'hands-on' and (from the management's point of view) starts to interfere. They feel as if the management team have not delivered their part of the contract. As a consequence they tend to fall back on what the subscription agreement says – in other words, they get legal. The balance of power effectively changes and for a while the venture capitalist seeks to run the business. Until net profit returns to planned levels, the management team will find life quite uncomfortable – but hopefully this will help them focus their efforts. However, the management team are still running the business and everything the venture capitalist does is perceived by them to be for the benefit of the business and in support of the management team.

Getting rid of an equity investor

As mentioned earlier, the wedding between venture capitalist and management is destined to be dissolved. Right from the start both parties need to be agreed on:

- when the business will be sold
- whom the business will be sold to

This may come as a surprise to you – but it shouldn't. If the business were taking out a loan it would be perfectly clear as to when it would be repaid and how. The venture capitalist has a right to receive payback at some predictable time in the future.

Some years ago I saw a TV programme that was part of a fly-on-the-wall series looking at how a particular venture-capital business worked. The bit I found really interesting was the 'beauty parade' during which they interviewed the owner-manager of a small publishing business. The venture-capital team asked him what his plans were for the business if he was given the money he was asking for. His reply was very clear and given with hardly a pause. In essence, he said, that he wanted to make the business very profitable, and sell it to a trade buyer when it was at its highest value in 3–5 years' time. He wanted then to use his share of the money to start a new business – with a totally different product and market. As he made this statement you could see the venture-capital team visibly beaming with joy. What they heard was music to their ears because if they invested in this business the management were committed to the same exit route as they wanted.

The exit route is very much determined by one factor: has the business performed according to plan (success) or has it underperformed (failure)?

Underperforming business

If a business has continued to underperform over a period of years then the venture capitalist will usually want to cut their losses and unload their investment for the best price they can get. They will not hold on to an investment just to be bloody-minded (regardless of what you may have heard). The business will be sold either to the incumbent management or a trade buyer. However, realistically, it is unlikely that the management of a poorly performing business will be able to raise enough money to buy out the venture capitalist. It is more likely that a competitor (trade buyer) will be found to buy the business. They will pay a higher price because they will consolidate the business into theirs, make cost savings and generally aim to turn the business around. If no trade buyer can be found then the venture capitalist will almost accept any price to get out – in which case the management team will be able to buy back the business.

Performing business

If the business has met its business plan objectives, especially its profit objectives, then a wider range of exit routes is possible. The dream of many people is to float their business on either the full stock market or the alternative investment market (AIM). It does not have to sell all its equity – just sufficient to buy out the previous investor. This route usually gets the best price – but only if the business is very profitable (established business) or can demonstrate potential profit (new business). However, this is by far and away the least likely exit route. The most common exit route is to sell the business on to another business – usually in the same industry (or complementary) and frequently a larger competitor. This can be a fairly quick process but generally yields a lower price than a public offering. The least likely exit route is a share repurchase by the management. If the business has performed to plan the buy-back price would usually be too high for the management to fund.

Time scale

Most people believe that this is a long-term relationship. In fact it is relatively short term, usually 3–5 years. This means that at some time after 2–3 years the venture-capital partner will be looking to sell the business on – assuming it is successful. However, do not discount the possibility of having a venture-capital partner for longer than this. If a business needs multiple investments as it grows then it may be 5–7 years before the business is saleable. In this case the venture capitalist will want a return on their money during this prolonged period.

Where can I get further help?

You should look at the following:

- The British Venture Capital Association (BVCA) Directory (published annually). BVCA, Essex House, 12–13 Essex Street, London WC2 3AA.
- Read *The Best-Laid Business Plans* by Paul Barrow (Virgin Publishing, 2001).

FAQ 23

'What other longer-term funding options could be open to my business?'

What do I need to know?

There is a truism that says you match funding to the need – in fact this was very clearly shown in the 'old-fashioned' style of balance sheet illustrated below:

Balance sheet @ 31/12/2000

Share capital	80,000	Fixed assets:	
Reserves	100,000	Land and buildings	110,000
Shareholders' funds	180,000	Plant and machinery	70,000
		Motor vehicles	20,000
Long-term loans	20,000		200,000
Current liabilities:		Current assets:	
Trade creditors	10,000	Debtors	20,000
Bank overdraft	20,000	Stock and WIP	10,000
	30,000		30,000
Total financing	230,000	Total assets	230,000

In this example we can see that long-term funding (shares, reserves and long-term debt (£200,000)) seems to have funded the long-term (fixed) assets (land and buildings, plant and machinery and motor vehicles (£200,000)). Also, we can see that short-term funding (trade creditors and bank overdraft (£30,000)) seems to have funded the short-term assets (debtors and stock and WIP (£30,000)). But nothing fundamentally has changed (apart from the way we present balance sheets), and this is how we should look at funding today.

What are the options?

Equity
The use of shares is known as equity funding and is particularly suited to raising large amounts. If you need to raise above, say, £250,000, then going outside the business to raise equity is an option. This can be done by going to a specialist equity provider, known as a venture-capital provider. Below this level of funding it is not cost-effective to take this route – although there are some specialist equity providers who may be able to meet this need.

For sums up to around £100,000, a private equity deal could be arranged with, say, a business angel. These are high-wealth individuals who invest in businesses in which they can have some management involvement as well as a return on their investment. For very large funding, then, what is known as a public offering or placing is possible on either the alternative investment market (AIM) or the stock exchange via a full listing. This is of course very time-consuming and costly, and does require a successful trading track record. Consequently, it is suitable only for raising millions of pounds.

Of course, this type of funding has a long-term cost to the business. These shareholders will want dividends for as long as they own their shares – which could be a lot longer than a bank loan. Also, dividends are not allowable against tax as a funding cost (unlike loan interest). Another point to be remembered when issuing shares is that your business must be valued so that a price can be worked out for the new shares being issued. This can be a contentious process with existing shareholders wanting as high a price as possible for 'diluting' their ownership of the business and potential buyers wanting as low a price as possible. And finally, remember that you have to be a limited company to issue shares – sorry, sole traders and partnerships!

Debenture

While we are looking at sources of funding available only to limited companies, we should also mention debentures. This is a bond, acknowledging a loan to the company, which bears a fixed rate of interest. This interest is payable regardless of whether profits are made or not (unlike shares). The debenture can either be redeemable (at some future agreed date) or irredeemable, in which case redemption will take place only when the company is eventually liquidated.

To increase the level of security to the lender under a debenture, a charge may be granted over all or certain assets to a debenture holder. In the case of non-payment of interest, the debenture holder can seize these assets and dispose of them to pay the outstanding interest. This is known as a mortgage debenture, whereas those debentures that do not have this right are known as naked or simple debentures.

Commercial mortgage

This is the business equivalent to the type of mortgage that millions of people within the UK use to buy their homes. A commercial mortgage can be used to buy business premises but is normally repayable within 10–15 years. Interest rates are usually fixed at the outset of the mortgage. The lender (usually a bank) has a first charge over the business premises being purchased. This means that in cases of non-payment of interest or capital the mortgagor (the lender) can call in the loan from the mortgagee (borrower), which generally means selling off the property to repay the loan. This type of loan is available to all types of businesses.

Shorter-term funding

Smaller fixed assets, such as motor vehicles, and current assets, such as debtors and stock, may also need funding. However, these require a shorter-term funding solution because their cycle of change is typically short-term – the motor vehicles every 3–4 years, and the stock and WIP on a constant cycle of change. Motor vehicles are frequently funded by long-term debt – hire purchase – and the stock and debtors funded by overdraft. Let's have a look at the main options open for short-term funding.

Bank loan or overdraft

This is probably the most common way of funding the majority of smaller UK businesses. Obviously, a bank loan is repayable over a fixed period and an overdraft is a continuous facility. It would, however, be wrong to think that an overdraft is not repayable. It is usually subject to an annual review and the bank has a right to ask for it to be repaid immediately if it wishes. Bank loans and overdrafts are usually quite easy and quick to arrange.

Overdrafts have interest charged at a rate linked to the bank's base rate – typically between 1 per cent and 5 per cent – which means of course that they can fluctuate in cost. There has been a tendency in recent years for banks to convert 'hard-core' overdrafts in to medium-term loans (say 3–5 years) as a way of reducing a business's indebtedness. These short-term bank loans are typically used to fund small asset purchases and the bank overdraft used to fund working capital (stock, debtors etc.). Both these options are open to all types of businesses.

You may be interested to know that bank managers have come under pressure in recent years to improve the quality of their lending. They now manage their portfolios more closely and will try to keep what they regard as poorer deals off their books. Do not be surprised if they offer other means of funding, such as hire purchase, leasing, factoring etc., which can be arranged by other associated businesses of their bank. This helps them to help you while keeping the risk off their books.

Small Firms Loan Guarantee Scheme

I know that we have already covered bank loans earlier, but a major problem that prevents many small businesses from getting a loan is security – or, more correctly, lack of it. A loan is arranged with a bank in the traditional way but is arranged under this scheme, which means that the Department of Trade and Industry (DTI) guarantee it. It is specifically available to most small and medium-sized businesses that have a viable business proposition but do not have adequate security to get bank funding. It is available for loans from £5,000 to £250,000 over periods of two to ten years and for most business purposes. The DTI will guarantee to pay the lending bank up to 85 per cent of the outstanding loan if the borrower fails to repay. However, this type of loan cannot be used to repay existing funding – it is only to be used for additional funding.

Arrangement fees are payable and a premium on the guaranteed part of the loan is payable to the DTI. The high street banks administer this scheme – so approach your bank. Obviously you will need to put forward your case (this business plan will help) and convince your bank. Loans up to £30,000 can be authorised immediately by the bank – above that a second independent manager within the bank will need to authorise the deal and it will be sent to the DTI for approval (usually rubber-stamping). Available for all type of businesses and something that you should seriously consider as part of your funding strategy.

Hire purchase, leasing and contract hire

Hire purchase (HP), leasing and contract hire are ways of acquiring assets such as cars and equipment, when the business does not wish to (or cannot) use a bank overdraft or bank loan. Under an HP agreement the business is contracting to buy the asset over an agreed period of years. To this extent it is similar to a term loan, except that the rate of interest paid will usually be higher and there will be penalties for early repayment of the loan. At the end of the HP contract, the asset belongs to the business.

Under a lease or contract hire, the business contracts to rent (not own) the asset over an agreed period of time – usually its useful life. It is responsible for maintaining the asset and returning it in good condition at the end of the period. There are penalties for early cancellation of the contract and at its end the asset will usually be required to be returned to its owner. An element of profit will be included in the rental cost so this will also cost more than a bank loan.

Under HP, leasing and contract hire a deposit is usually required and in some cases a final substantial payment may be required. Leases and contract-hire payments are subject to VAT and are allowable against the profit of the business. These are often referred to as 'off-balance-sheet financing' – because since you are not buying the asset it does not show on the balance sheet as either an asset or a liability. All these options are open to all types of businesses.

Grants and awards

Your business may be located in a region that has been identified for special support. This Regional Selective Assistance (RSA) is aimed at giving discretionary grants to businesses that want to relocate or expand in these areas for projects that create new jobs or protect existing jobs. Examples of this support are: REG (Regional Enterprise Grants) to smaller businesses to support capital projects up to 15 per cent of the costs (up to a limit of £15,000) are available. The Rural Development Commission (RDC) may be able to give grants to convert redundant buildings. In addition 'soft' loans are available under the Small Firms Training Loan scheme and Career Development Loans scheme.

Other support is aimed specifically at businesses involved in innovation and technology. These awards are not dependent on geographical location. Examples of these are:

- **SMART Award**, which is worth up to £45,000 for businesses with up to 50 employees to support innovative technology.
- **SPUR Award**, which is worth up to ECU 200,000 for businesses with up to 250 employees to support significant technology advance.
- **TCS (Teaching Company Scheme)** which will help most small businesses obtain the use of a graduate for up to two years for about 30 per cent of the real cost.

A business can apply for all these grants – they are not mutually exclusive. My friend Andrew Waterfall, who runs Improvision, has had all of these. Again, a business plan is required and you must remember that these are effectively competitions because there is a limited pot of money to be awarded. Remember:

- Most grants are awarded throughout the year: so there is generally no cut-off dates for applications – unless a grant is coming to an end. Most grants are specifically targeted to alleviate

> unemployment and available to businesses in designated geographical areas.
>
> ■ Some awards are annual competitions, so there are cut-off dates for applications. Some may be held once or more than once a year. In some cases there are various stages to the competitions. However, to be successful your business must be highly innovative and technology based.

In summary, there are a wide range of funding options for both long-term and short-term needs – in fact the array of options can be quite bewildering. Do look carefully at each of these options to see if they may be appropriate to your needs. If you need to find out more about any of these, look in the appendices for contact details – but be aware that grants and awards come in and out of favour, so check to see if the one you're interested in is still available.

Where can I get further help?

You should look at the following:

> ■ Contact your accountant, financial adviser, or the Factors and Discounters Association (020 8332 9955).
>
> ■ 'My bank manager won't increase my overdraft – what other options are there?' FAQ 9
>
> ■ Free help on grants and awards is available from your local Business Link or the Department of Trade and Industry (DTI) (020 7215 5000 for General Enquiries).

CHAPTER FOUR

Questions on financial statements

 FAQ 24

'How do I make sense of the balance sheet?'

What do I need to know?

An awful lot of mystery surrounds the balance sheet – mostly created by accountants. It's almost as if the accountants are trying to create a language of their own so that they can exclude the rest of the world. That's a shame, really, because the balance sheet is an incredibly simple financial statement, which anyone can understand. It's one of the holy trinity of financial statements – the others being the profit and loss statement and the cash flow forecast.

The balance sheet is a 'snapshot' of the business at a point in time (usually the financial year end) and shows:

> ■ where the business got its money from
> ■ where the business spent it
> ■ the time perspective for each of these – either short or long

That's it in simple terms but we accountants have managed to make it more difficult by devising a language all of our own. The framework below shows how this all looks.

The section of the balance sheet that shows '**where the business got its money from**' is called 'financing' and is referred to as liabilities – because the business has acquired this money from outsiders, who

Balance Sheet @ 31/12/2000

Where the business got its money from	Where the business spent it
Long term	Long term
Short term	Short term

will want it back sometime. These outsiders are shareholders and providers of long-term debt and they provide (as their name suggests) long-term financing. On a short-term basis a business can obtain financing from trade creditors, the tax man, the VAT man etc. These are referred to as current liabilities.

The other side shows '**where the business spent it**' and these are referred to as assets – either fixed or current. Fixed assets are those that we buy solely so that we can carry out our business – land and buildings, plant and machinery, motor vehicles etc. They stay in the business for a long time. Current assets are those that are constantly changing – stock, debtors, cash. They stay in the business for a short time.

That is the broad outline of the balance sheet – all we need to do now is actually look at one with some numbers in it and fill in some of the details and understand some key underlying concepts.

An example with some numbers

The balance sheet below shows the state of affairs for a company called Precision Engineering Ltd as at 31 December 2000. It has been presented in what is known as the 'side-by-side' format: the assets and liabilities are shown side by side. While this style is not in common use now, it does help us to understand the balance sheet better.

Precision Engineering Ltd – Balance Sheet @ 31/12/2000

Where we got the money from

Long term

Shareholders' funds		
Share capital	10,000	
Reserves	45,700	
		55,700

Long-term loans > 12 months		
Hire purchase	1,000	
Director's loan	10,000	
Mortgage	15,000	
		26,000

Short Term
Current liabilities < 12 months

PAYE/NI/VAT etc.	1,000	
Trade creditors	5,000	
Accruals	500	
Bank overdraft	5,000	
		11,500

Total liabilities | 93,200 |

Where we spent it

Long term

NBV

Fixed assets (or tangible assets)		
Land and buildings (1%)	30,000	
Plant and machinery (20%)	10,000	
Fixtures and fittings (25%)	3,000	
		43,000

Intangible assets		
Goodwill	20,000	
R&D	10,000	
Patents, trade marks etc.	5,000	
		35,000

Short term
Current assets

Stock and WIP	5,000	
Debtors	10,000	
Prepayments	200	
Bank balance	0	
		15,200

Total assets | 93,200 |

Before we start to look at the specifics of this balance sheet let's introduce some general concepts and conventions.

VAT (Value Added Tax)

As a general rule all figures shown in the balance sheet are shown exclusive of VAT, except for trade creditors and debtors. For example, when you sell a customer goods for £100 and add the £17.50 of VAT (17.5 per cent), how much are you owed by your customer? The full £117.50. And that's what we show in the balance sheet – the same principle applies for trade creditors.

Money measurement

Only items that can be measured in money terms are included in the balance sheet. This means we do not include things such as the loyalty of our customers and staff, the location of our business, the health of the managing director. These may all have an impact on the business but they do not have a monetary value.

Cost concept

Assets are included at either original cost or net realisable value, whichever is the lower. The reason for this is that over time an asset will reduce in value (depreciate) as a result of constant use, the passing of time and obsolescence.

Business entity

Financial statements (including the balance sheet) are kept for the business and show transactions from its point of view. For example, if a director lends the business £10,000 (as in Precision Engineering Ltd) this is shown as a liability because the business owes that money and will have to pay it back sometime. However, from the director's point of view he will view this as an asset, because someone (the business) owes him.

Going concern

There is an underlying assumption that the business will continue trading in the future. Based on this assumption all assets are valued on a going-concern basis – i.e., they will be used to generate profit in the normal course of business. If, however, the business was due to close down in a few weeks' time, then a completely different valuation would be placed on the same assets: it would be what they could realise on the open market. This would be a much lower figure.

Dual aspect

We need to show both sides of all transactions within the balance sheet: i.e. 'where it came from' and 'where it went'. So, for example, if the directors had invested £10,000 in the business to help buy the land and buildings, we would see both sides of this transaction as:

Liability – £10,000 share capital introduced by the directors.
Assets – £10,000 land and buildings (part of the full value) paid for by the directors.

Conservatism

Accountants must err on the side of caution – i.e. include assets at their lowest value and show profits at their lowest value. This does not mean that they should deliberately understate assets and profit but that they should use values that will stand up to scrutiny.

Consistency

Accountants are tasked with showing a 'true and fair' view. To help achieve this they should be consistent in the manner in which they treat items from one period to the next. For example, if one year they decide that all items under £1,000 in cost will be treated as revenue items (i.e. expenses against profit) then that is how it should stay. It would be inconsistent if in a later period they decided to treat some items below £1,000 as capital (i.e. not as expenses against profit, but as an asset) just because the expenditure was on small items of fixtures and fittings, which could also be classified as assets in the balance sheet.

Armed with these rules of the game, let's quickly go round the balance sheet to explain what we see (using Precision Engineering Ltd) as our model.

Top left: where we got the money from – long term

In this area we are concentrating on the long-term funding of the business. These are:

- **Shareholders' capital** – the first people to give their money to the business. They will get their money back only when the company is sold/liquidated. There is no guarantee that they will get back what they put in. Their expectations are: (a) dividends (when times are good), and (b) for the shares to go up in value. In bad times they get nothing.
- **Reserves** – these belong to the shareholders and represent all the years of profit that they have chosen to leave in the business, which could have been taken out as dividends.
- **Long-term liabilities** – for some strange accounting reason long-term means anything longer than twelve months. These are the people who have lent their money to the business. They will get their money back, with interest, by instalments according to their agreement. Whether times are good or bad they expect their payments on time. In good times they get no more than: shareholders' capital + reserves + long-term liabilities = capital employed. Also of interest is the relationship between shareholders' funds and long-term liabilities, which is known as gearing (and is covered in FAQ 31).

Bottom left: where we got the money from – short term

In this area we are concentrating on the short-term funding of the business. This is collectively known as current liabilities because they are due for repayment within the next twelve months:

- **PAYE/NI/VAT etc.** – these are the various taxes and levies that a business collects on behalf of the Inland Revenue and HM Customs and Excise. For example, if a business is VAT-registered then it collects this from its customers (when it gets paid) and can keep it in its own bank account for up to three months (depending on how quickly it gets paid and when its quarterly return is due). This is effectively an interest-free short-term loan.

- **Trade creditors** – these are your suppliers, who give you credit when you buy goods/services from them. In effect they are funding your business for 30 or 60 days (depending on when you pay them). If you take too long to pay them they get unhappy (see FAQ 7).

- **Accruals** – an accrual is where you recognise a charge for some goods or service that you have used but for which you have not as yet received an invoice (e.g., the quarterly telephone account, where you make calls each month but receive a bill quarterly in arrears). To make sure the cost of these calls is taken into the correct accounting period an accrual (or charge) is made for these calls each period.

- **Bank overdraft** – fairly self-explanatory, but note that overdrafts are repayable on demand. It is therefore a short-term funding option, although most small businesses regard it as part of their long-term funding.

Top right: where we spent the money – long term

In this area we are concentrating on the long-term assets that the business has bought and that are needed to run the business and will be retained for as long as the business continues:

Fixed assets

These are what I call the 'big lumps' that the business owns so it can remain in business. Typically these include land and buildings, plant and machinery, fixtures and fittings, motor vehicles. These are shown at net book value (NBV), which is original cost less accumulated depreciation. Do note that assets that are leased or rented to not appear on the balance sheet because the business does not own them – this is known as off-balance-sheet financing.

Intangible assets

This is another category of long-term asset, which is uncommon in most small businesses but features in larger companies. I have to say that I am a little rude about these and often refer to them as 'Mickey

Mouse' assets, because they do not physically exist. I also have to say that bank managers have even less enthusiasm for them than I do! In reality, intangible assets are deferred expenditure (i.e., they are really business expenses that should, and will some day, be written of in the profit and loss statement against profit). However, accounting standards permit them to exist for a while. Let's have a look at some specific examples of intangible assets.

■ **Goodwill** – often misunderstood, but technically exists only in the balance sheet of a business that has bought another business. Goodwill is the difference between what you pay for a business over and above the value of the net assets. In effect it is the amount that you have paid 'over the odds' to buy that business. Accounting standards demand that it should be written off as quickly as possible against available profits.

■ **Research and development** – this is where a business has spent money, usually over several years, to create new products and services, which will at some time in the future yield profitable sales (hopefully). Because no sales have yet to come in for these new products and services (they don't exist yet) the business can defer this expenditure until they do. In the meantime this accumulating spending of money is allowed to remain in the balance sheet. When the products and services are ready for market this must be written off against profit.

■ **Patents and trade marks** – this is money spent by the business on creating and protecting products and their associates words, logos, images.

Bottom right: where we spent the money – short term

In this area we are concentrating on the current assets that the business has bought and created but that will be quickly converted into cash:

Stock and work in progress (WIP)

These are those goods that the business has bought from its suppliers and worked on and that will finally become finished goods (or services) that will be sold on to customers.

Debtors

These are those customers that you have sold your goods and services to but who have not as yet paid you.

Prepayments

A prepayment is where you pay in advance for some goods or service that you have not used, e.g., the quarterly telephone account, where you pay in advance for the next quarter's line rental. To make sure the cost of the line rental is taken into the correct accounting period a prepayment is made for this in each period.

Bank balance

Fairly self-explanatory, this represents the value held in the business bank account. Note that this may be different from that shown on the bank statement, owing to cheques issued and cheques received that have not yet hit the bank. Each month businesses do what is called a 'bank reconciliation' to compare what the business believes the bank balance to be with that shown by the bank.

Summary

When you look at the balance sheet using the above approach, it really is quite straightforward in what it tells us; it is perhaps some of the detail that may be unknown. The balance sheet we have looked at in this FAQ was in the older style. You can see the same balance sheet using the more modern presentation style in the Appendix.

Where can I get further help?

You should look at the following:

- Contact your accountant.
- Read *Business Accounting*, 1 and 2, by Frank Wood (Pitman Publishing, 1996).
- Read the other FAQs referred to in the text.

FAQ 25

'What does the profit and loss statement tell me about a business?'

What do I need to know?

Fortunately, the profit and loss statement is mostly quite straight-forward – in both its layout and content. The profit and loss statement shows the changing picture of the business over a period of time, normally twelve months (but could and should be more frequent than that). It shows:

> ■ the trading position of the business – what profit (or loss) the business has made during the period
>
> ■ the key figures such as sales, cost of sales, gross margin etc.

That is the broad outline of the profit and loss statement – all we need to do now is to actually look at one with some numbers in it and fill in some of the details and understand some key underlying concepts.

An example with some numbers

The profit and loss statement below shows the trading position of a company called Precision Engineering Ltd. It is common practice for a business to prepare its profit and loss account (statement) in a form that is most suitable to their business.

Before we start to look at the specifics of this profit and loss account let's introduce some general concepts and conventions.

> ■ **VAT (Value Added Tax):** All figures shown in the profit and loss account (statement) are shown exclusive of VAT.
>
> ■ **Realisation concept:** Sales income should be taken into the profit statement only when it has been earned. It is not earned at the point the order is received – it is earned only when the goods (or services) have been dispatched and invoiced. If your business is one where goods are often returned and this can be estimated accurately (perhaps based on historical trends), then an adjustment can be made to sales income.
>
> ■ **Accrual concept:** The profit statement should match income and expenditure from the same period. It is only by doing this that a correct measure of profit can be determined. An adjustment, called an accrual or a prepayment, is made to ensure that costs are taken into the correct time period (see FAQ 24 for examples of accruals and prepayments).

The key elements of this profit statement are:

Precision Engineering Ltd

Profit and loss account for the 12 months ended 31/12/00

Sales		**150,000**
Cost of sales:		
– Opening stock	20,000	
– Purchases	70,000	
	90,000	
Less closing stock	–25,000	
Cost of sales		**65,000**
Gross profit		**85,000**
Operating expenses:		
Rent and rates	15,000	
Heat and light	3,000	
Telephone	1,500	
Professional fees	2,000	
Employee costs	50,000	
Stationery and advertising	1,200	
Depreciation	800	
		73,500
Operating (or trading) profit		**11,500**
Non-operating income:		
Dividends received	400	
Rent	1,000	
		1,400
		12,900
Financing costs:		
Loan interest		2,200
Net profit before tax		**10,700**
Provision for Tax (20%)		2,140
Net profit after tax		**8,560**

The headings and figures in **bold** are worthy of explanation:

■ **Sales** – the net sales for the period after all adjustments for credit notes, sales return reserves etc. This is the trading income of the business. Note that if goods and services are sold on credit then all of these sales will not necessarily have been paid for.

■ **Cost of sales** – the cost of those sales made during the period. The problem arises where the purchases figure shown (in this case £70,000) has not all been used within the period, which is very likely. For example, deliveries of materials received during the last weeks and days will almost certainly remain unused in stock. To make sure that the correct cost of sales figure is arrived at, an adjustment is made for the differences between closing stock at the end of this period (closing stock) and the closing stock at the end of the previous period (opening stock).

- **Gross profit** – also frequently referred to as gross margin. This is the difference between sales and cost of sales. However, it is more significant than the calculation suggests. Gross profit is the key measure of business performance. It measures what I call the 'engine of the business' and shows how much a business makes out of its key activity – making (or buying in) goods and service for resale. It is a measure of core activity before the remaining non-productive costs are taken into account.

- **Operating expenses** – all the normal business expenses incurred in running the business but excluding all financing costs.

- **Operating (or trading) profit** – the difference between gross profit and operating expenses. An important measure of trading performance because it shows how profitable a business is before taking into account the financing costs.

- **Financing costs** – costs related to the financing or funding of the business. Includes items such as hire purchase and loan interest.

- **Net profit before tax** – shows how much profit (or loss) the business has made after all business costs but before any tax has been allowed for.

- **Net profit after tax** – shows how much profit (or loss) the business has made after all costs, including tax.

As already stated, there is a great deal of flexibility in the way small businesses prepare their accounts, especially if they are sole traders or partnerships. However, limited companies have to prepare accounts and file them with the Registrar of Companies in a more prescribed format according to company size (see FAQ 27).

Where can I get further help?

You should look at the following:

- Contact your accountant.
- Read *Business Accounting*, 1 and 2, by Frank Wood (Pitman Publishing, 1996).
- Read the other FAQs referred to in the text.

FAQ 26

'What does the cash flow forecast tell me about a business?'

What do I need to know?

The purpose of the cash flow forecast is to provide a prediction (looking forward) of how well a business will generate cash and the effect it will have on the bank balance during the forecast period (not necessarily a year). The key features of the cash flow forecast are:

> ■ It shows cash inflow and outflow on a monthly basis.
> ■ It does not distinguish between revenue and capital.
> ■ Its objective is to show the months in which cash flows lead to the bank balance becoming negative.

That is the broad outline of the cash flow forecast – all we need to do now is actually look at one with some numbers in it and fill in some of the details and understand some key underlying concepts.

An example with some numbers

You have been given the following information about Lowfields, a start-up business. Its profit forecast is as shown below:

Lowfields

Profit forecast for the 6 months to 31/12/00

Sales		60,000
Cost of sales (purchases)		18,000
Gross profit		42,000
Expenses:		
Rent	12,000	
Rates	3,000	
Wages	6,000	
Advertising	3,000	
Depreciation	2,500	
Loan interest	135	
		26,635
Net profit		15,365

The following additional information is available about the business:

- Please ignore VAT – although this business would need to be registered for VAT it has been ignored to keep this example as simple as possible. The VAT registration threshold changes each year in the budget but in 2000 it was £52,000 per annum.

- Sales during Month 1 will be £5,000 and grow by £2,000 per month to a maximum of £15,000 in Month 6.

- The business will be paid two months in arrears by its debtors for any sales made.

- Purchases (cost of sales) are a constant 30 per cent of sales and are paid for during the month of purchase.

- Rent is paid quarterly in advance from Month 1.

- Rates are paid by ten equal instalments starting in Month 1.

- Wages are paid evenly throughout the six months.

- An advertising campaign will start and be paid for in Month 1 and be continued in Months 3 and 5.

- A new machine will be purchased for cash in Month 1 at a cost of £20,000. It will be depreciated at a rate of 25 per cent per annum.

- A bank loan of £5,000 has been secured during Month 1. This will be repayable over 36 months (starting in Month 1) with interest being paid monthly at a rate of 10 per cent.

- There is £2,000 in the bank account at the start of Month 1.

Based on the profit forecast the business looks to be quite healthy and certainly strong enough to support the bank loan of £5,000 – but how will its cash flow forecast look?

Looking at the cash flow forecast below we see a somewhat different picture. In fact a business that shows a profit of over £15,000 actually shows a bank balance declining from £2,000 to just £434 during the same period. However, the cash flow forecast shows things to be even worse than that. From Month 1 to Month 5 there is a need for additional funding (over and above the £5,000 the bank has lent and the £20,000 the owner put in) – in fact during Month 4 some £8,644 additional finance is needed.

Lowfields

Cash flow forecast for the 6 months to 31/12/00

	Month 1	Month 2	Month 3	Month 4	Month 5	Month 6
Receipts:						
Debtor payments	0	0	5,000	7,000	9,000	11,000
Owner's capital	20,000					
Bank loan	5,000					
Total cash receipts	25,000	0	5,000	7,000	9,000	11,000
Payments:						
New machine	20,000					
Purchases	1,500	2,100	2,700	3,300	3,900	4,500
Rent	6,000			6,000		
Rates	600	600	600	600	600	600
Wages	1,000					
Advertising	1,000		1,000		1,000	
Loan repayments	161	161	161	161	161	161
Total cash payments	30,261	2,861	4,461	10,061	5,661	5,261
Net cash flow for month	−5,261	−2,861	539	−3,061	3,339	5,739
Opening bank balance	2,000	−3,261	−6,122	−5,583	−8,644	−5,305
Closing bank balance	−3,261	−6,122	−5,583	−8,644	−5,305	434

This shows the purpose of the cash flow forecast to very good effect. Based on this picture, if I was the owner of Lowfields, I would want to do the cash flow forecast through to the end of the year just to make sure that the business is capable of funding its own cash flow requirements.

Where can I get further help?

You should look at the following:

- Contact your accountant.
- Read *Business Accounting*, 1 and 2, by Frank Wood (Pitman Publishing, 1996).
- Read the other FAQs referred to in the text.

FAQ 27

'What is the difference between statutory accounting and management accounting?'

What do I need to know?

Throughout the FAQs in this book you will see financial statements, such as the balance sheet and profit and loss account. In general these have been prepared for internal use and would normally be referred to as management accounts. As long as they comply with the accounting conventions they can be set out in any way the user wants – usually in a format that helps them the most. However, **limited companies** have to produce these financial statements for statutory purposes as well, which is essentially for external use: the Registrar of Companies, shareholders and the Inland Revenue. In these cases the accounts prepared have to comply with set-out formats, which vary according to the size of the business – the bigger the company the more onerous the information requirement. Because these accounts are for use by parties outside the business, additional supporting information is required, such as the directors' report, and either an accountants' report or auditors' report. Statutory accounts are not user-friendly.

Definition of small and medium-sized companies

Special exemptions apply to small and medium-sized companies that simplify (and restrict) the amount of reporting that applies to them. The following criteria are laid down to define these two categories of company. A company will be treated as a small or medium-sized company if it does not exceed more than one of the following criteria:

	Small	Medium-sized
Turnover (sales)	£2.8 million	£11.2 million
Balance sheet total (gross assets)	£1.4 million	£5.6 million
Average number of employees (full time)	50	250

These criteria are subject to change periodically, so please make sure that when you read this you check that this information is still current.

Exemptions for small companies

Small companies are entitled to certain exemptions:

 Annual accounts for shareholders – can prepare modified balance sheet and other reduced disclosure requirements for the notes to the accounts and the directors' report.

- Abbreviated accounts for filing and delivery to the Registrar of Companies (see less detailed balance sheet below).
- Exemption from the statutory requirement to have their annual accounts audited if annual turnover is below £350,000.

Here is an example of a less detailed balance sheet (permissible for small companies) – it must show the following headings, known as Format 1 (modified):

Balance sheet set out under Format 1

CALLED-UP SHARE CAPITAL NOT PLAYED

FIXED ASSETS

Intangible assets
Goodwill
Other intangible assets

Tangible assets
Land and buildings
Plant and machinery etc.

Investments
Shares in group companies
Loans to group companies
Other investments (excluding loans)
Others (including loans)

CURRENT ASSETS
Stocks
Payments on account

Debtors
Trade debtors
Intergroup debts
Others

Investments
Shares in group companies
Other investments

Cash at bank and in hand

PREPAYMENTS AND ACCRUED INCOME

CREDITORS: amounts due within one year
Bank loans and overdrafts
Trade creditors
Loans from group companies

Other creditors

NET CURRENT ASSETS (LIABILITIES)

TOTAL ASSETS LESS CURRENT LIABILITIES

CREDITORS: amounts due after more than one year
Bank loans and overdrafts
Trade creditors
Loans from group companies
Other creditors

PROVISIONS FOR LIABILITIES AND CHARGES

ACCRUALS AND DEFERRED INCOME

CAPITAL AND RESERVES
Called-up share capital
Share premium account
Revaluation reserve
Other reserves
Profit and loss account

Filing abbreviated accounts

A small company can submit to the Registrar of Companies what is known as abbreviated accounts. Medium-sized companies are also entitled to submit abbreviated accounts and the comparison between the two is shown in the table below.

	Small	Medium-sized
Directors' report	No report	Full report
Profit and loss account	Not required	Required – but may start from 'gross profit'
Balance sheet	Abbreviated version	Full balance sheet
Funds flow statement	Not required	Full statements required
Notes to accounts	Limited information only No information on directors' or employees' emoluments	Full notes, except particulars of turnover are omitted
Auditors' report	Special report	Special report
Accountants' report	Special report	Not available

Exemptions for medium-sized companies

Medium-sized businesses are required to prepare and file essentially full accounts, apart from the profit and loss account exemption on disclosing turnover (as shown in the table above). They can prepare and submit a profit and loss account in what is known as Format 1 shown below.

Example of a less detailed profit and loss account (permissible for medium-sized companies)

Profit and loss account set out under Format 1

Turnover (can be omitted for medium-sized companies)
Cost of sales (can be omitted for medium-sized companies)
Gross profit or loss
Distribution costs
Administration expenses
Other operating income
Income from shares in group companies
Income from other group activities or:
a. Income from interests in associated undertakings
b. Income from other participating interests
Income from other fixed asset investments
Other interest receivable and similar income
Amounts written off investments
Interest payable and similar charges
Tax on profit or loss on ordinary activities
Profit or loss on ordinary activities after taxation
Minority interests
Extraordinary charges
Extraordinary profit or loss
Other taxes not shown under the above items
Profit or loss for the financial year

Note: Depreciation and other amounts written off tangible and intangible fixed assets must be disclosed in a note.

Summary

Statutory accounts are prepared to a standard format – there are two different formats for balance sheets and four different formats for profit and loss accounts. They do not take into account any industry or trade requirements – it's a case of complying with the statutory requirements. As such they do not make any pretence at being 'user-friendly' and accessible to non-accountants. Their sole purpose is to provide the same information for all businesses in exactly the same format.

Where can I get further help?

You should look at the following:

- Contact your accountant.
- Read *Business Accounting*, 1 and 2, by Frank Wood (Pitman Publishing, 1996).
- Read *Preparing Company Accounts* by Accountancy Books (1994).

CHAPTER FIVE

Questions on business control

FAQ 28

'How can using ratios help me manage my business better?'

What do I need to know?

If you are running a business, how do you know whether it is doing well? On its own a piece of information like sales or gross profit could be of only limited use. The fact that this year's sales in your business have been, say, £150,000 and gross profit £50,000 does not on its own say good or bad to me. However, we need to look at:

1. **The relationship between key financial figures** (both in the profit and loss account and the balance sheet) – which is called ratio analysis. A key example would be debtor days, which measures how long a business takes (on average) to collect its debts. Then ...

2. **Compare these ratios over a period of time** – which we call trends, to see how a business has done over recent years. From this you may be able to see a pattern of underperformance in a key area and start to target remedial action. Then ...

3. **Compare these ratios with similar businesses** – which we call yardsticks, to see how a business compares with its key competitors. If it is growing slower and is less profitable than a competitor this may well spell danger.

By combining all three above we start to have a framework for monitoring a business, identifying where things are going wrong, and focus effort to improve business performance.

A few words of warning on the use of ratios

The use of ratios is not a perfect science. Sometimes the financial information that you really need is not available in statutory accounts. For example, if you want to calculate creditor days accurately you really need the purchases figure. Unfortunately, this will not be available, so using the cost-of-sales figure is an acceptable alternative (see FAQ 30). Just remember to be consistent in the way you calculate your ratios – from one year to another, and from one company to another. Also, if you sat twelve accountants in a room they would come up with twelve different ways of calculating the same ratio! Use and modify the ratios that are in this book – see what works for you.

There are some analysts who believe that you should 'average' ratios that involve balance sheet figures (stock, debtors, capital employed etc.) by taking the average of the opening and closing balance sheet figures. Their argument is that, during periods of high growth in a business, this smoothes or averages out some abnormalities in the resulting ratios. My experience is that, over a period of several years, this has little or no effect on the resulting trend or comparison with other businesses. Also when speaking to the leading banks, who are seriously into ratio analysis, they have confirmed that they do not average – it is an unnecessary complication.

What are the common business objectives?

All businesses have two common business objectives, which allow us to assess how well a business is doing.

Objective 1: To make a satisfactory return on its investment

All enterprises must make a satisfactory return or profit. For ,example if you had £10,000 that you wanted to invest, would you consider the return you are going to get as important? Of course you would. You would want the best return possible – and investing in and running a business should be no different. You want to make a good return in your business. To assess whether you are achieving this I would suggest that your return must meet the following criteria:

- **Fair return** to the shareholders/proprietor/partners. This of course needs to take into account the level of risk being taken. For example, a very low-risk investment (bank deposit) may offer a return of only 5 per cent, which may be considered as good. If your business is considerably more speculative and is offering a return of less than this, your investors will not be too pleased.

- **Sufficient profit** to permit growth. If you want to grow a business then it must make sufficient profit to offer a return for its investors (see above) and leave enough to provide for future working capital and capital projects. The more a business uses its own funds to grow (shareholders' funds), then the less it will have to borrow and the cheaper (and more profitable) growth will be.

- Good enough to attract **new investors**. Existing investors may be prepared to accept a low return (possibly because they can't realise their investment). But if the business is to attract new investment the return must be better than average.

- **Better than inflation**. Investors want to make sure that their capital remains intact. If inflation is currently running at 7 per cent and your business is offering a return of 5 per cent then your investors are effectively losing 2 per cent each year! You must do better than this if you wish to retain this investment.

Of course there are various factors that have an affect return on investment:

- Those that affect profit – so anything you can do to improve profit will automatically improve return (as long as you do not increase investment): e.g., increase sales, reduce costs etc.

- Those that affect investment – so if you can reduce the investment in the business this will also automatically improve return (so long as you do not reduce profit): e.g., dispose of fixed assets, working capital etc.

The schedule below shows the factors that affect 'return on capital employed' (ROCE), which is one of the ratios that we can use to measure return on investment. This shows the business as it is now.

Current position				
Profit:			**Investment:**	
Sales	60,000		Fixed assets	100,000
Cost of sales	18,000			
Gross profit	42,000			
Expenses	26,500		Net current assets	2,000
Operating profit	15,500			
Loan interest	135			
Net profit	15,365		Capital Employed	102,000
			$ROCE = \frac{15,365}{102,000} =$	15.06%

As it stands now the business is making a rather modest 15.06 per cent ROCE. Supposing the business decides to work on its profit to improve ROCE. The schedule below shows the effect increasing sales to £100,000 with the appropriate increase in cost of sales to £36,000 has had on net profit and therefore on ROCE.

Improving profit				
Profit:			**Investment:**	
Sales	100,000		Fixed assets	100,000
Cost of sales	36,000			
Gross profit	64,000			
Expenses	26,500		Net current assets	2,000
Operating profit	37,500			
Loan interest	135			
Net profit	37,365		Capital Employed	102,000
			$ROCE = \frac{37,365}{102,000} =$	36.63%

Now the business has improved ROCE to 36.63 per cent – more than doubled.

The final option (if profitability cannot be improved) is to reduce the capital employed by selling fixed assets or reducing the net current assets used in the business (debtors, stock etc.). The schedule below shows the effect of reducing fixed assets to £40,000 (i.e. selling £60,000 worth of fixed assets). This has the effect of reducing capital employed to £42,000, which has in turn improved ROCE.

Reducing investment

Profit:		Investment:	
Sales	60,000	Fixed assets	40,000
Cost of sales	18,000		
Gross profit	42,000		
Expenses	26,500	Net current assets	2,000
Operating profit	15,500		
Loan interest	135		
Net profit	15,365	Capital Employed	42,000

$$\text{ROCE} = \frac{15,365}{42,000} = \qquad 36.58\%$$

Now the business has improved ROCE to 36.58 per cent – again more than doubled.

Objective 2: To make sure the business remains sound

As well as making a satisfactory return, the business should be protected from unnecessary risk. There will be some business risks that the business cannot avoid (e.g., competitors reducing prices, new products, economic recession etc.). However, the management are responsible for making sure that risk does nothing to jeopardise the business's position (e.g., run out of cash, borrow too much money, run the risk of bad debts).

We will look at some ratios later that measure risk.

Using ratios

Financial analysis requires comparisons – we have already seen this in the ROCE calculation. This ratio gives a basic measure – but how do we know if it is good or bad? What we need are some yardsticks to give us a better idea if, say, our initial ROCE of 15.06 per cent is any good.

- **Personal (or business) goal.** If for example you had set a personal objective of 10 per cent for ROCE, then 15.06 per cent looks pretty good. Setting business goals is also known as budgeting (see later FAQs), and we can use ratios to set budgets and monitor actual business performance.

- **Comparison with last year.** If, for example, last year you achieved 20 per cent ROCE, then this year's figure of 15.06 per cent looks a bit sick by comparison. This tells us that the business is doing worse than last year.

■ **Comparison with other businesses.** It can be really useful to see how you compare with your competitors – if you do not perform as well as they do, then you run the risk of going out of business. Again, if the average ROCE for your competitors was 20 per cent then your figure of 15.06 per cent says that something is wrong – you are underperforming in comparison.

We have looked at only one ratio – ROCE – but there is a whole range that you can use, each of which focuses on a different aspect of the business.

Ratios are grouped according to what they focus on:

■ **Measures of profitability** tell us how good (or bad) the return has been for the key investors in the business (e.g., return on capital employed).

■ **Measures of trading performance**, as the name implies, tell us how well the business is trading in terms of profitability (e.g., gross profit percentage).

■ **Working capital (including liquidity and efficiency)** measures how well the business is managing its short-term assets and liabilities, a critical area (e.g., debtor days).

■ **Measures of growth** tell us how key figures have changed over the years (e.g., sales growth).

■ **Measures of risk (or solvency)**, as the name implies, tell us how well funded the business is (e.g., gearing).

Where can I get further help?

You should look at the following:

■ Read the other FAQs on business control.
■ Read *Business Accounting,* 1 and 2, by Frank Wood (Pitman Publishing, 1996).

FAQ 29

'What measures can I use to help monitor profitability?'

What do I need to know?

The main reason for being in business is to make profit. There are very few businesses where just existing is sufficient reason in itself.

However, the profit objective can, and should, be measured at two levels:

1. **Internal** – used to measure the performance of management to see how well they are managing the business. Includes the key measures such as gross profit percentage, operating/trading profit percentage etc.
2. **External** – used to measure how well the shareholders and other funding institutions have done out of the business. Includes the key measures such as return on shareholders' capital (ROSC), return on capital employed (ROCE).

This FAQ looks specifically at measures of trading performance (internal) and profitability (external), and explains how to use them and what they mean. We shall be using Mark Engineering Ltd (MEL) (see Appendix) as an example for the calculation of these ratios. Each of the ratios has been calculated for the years 2001 and 2000, and is given together with a brief commentary on any changes over these years.

Measures of trading performance (internal measures)

1. Gross profit to sales (gross profit percentage)
The gross profit percentage (GP per cent) expresses gross profit as a percentage of sales. This is one ratio that stands out head and shoulders above the rest – GP per cent. Many students of mine have left with the words 'GP per cent is the most important measure of business performance – it shows how well the engine of the business is performing' buzzing in their heads. All businesses make something (manufacturing business), perform a service (service business), or sell someone else's products (retail business). The primary objective must be to do this as well as possible – which is what the GP per cent does.

It is calculated as follows:

$$\text{Gross profit percentage (GP\%)} = \frac{\text{Gross profit}}{\text{Sales}} \times 100$$

$$\text{MEL 2001} \quad \text{GP\%} = \frac{105,055}{185,000} \times 100 = 56.78\%$$

$$\text{MEL 2000} \quad \text{GP\%} = \frac{85,500}{160,000} \times 100 = 53.44\%$$

Comment on MEL

GP% has improved from 53.44 per cent to 56.78 per cent, which is an improvement of nearly 6 per cent $\left(\dfrac{56.78\% - 53.44\%}{53.44\%} \times 100 \right)$.

This could be due to greater efficiency in any (or all) of the direct cost of sales elements – materials, heat and light, direct wages. It could also be due to a small increase in selling price.

How do I improve it?

Attack all the factors that affect gross profit (selling price, purchases, direct labour etc.). For more details on improving GP per cent, refer to FAQ 15.

2. Operating profit to sales (operating profit percentage)

The operating profit percentage expresses operating profit (sometimes also known as trading profit) as a percentage of sales. Shows how profitable the business is after all operating (or trading) expenses but before any financing costs (bank interest etc.). Operating profit percentage falls between GP per cent (see above) and net profit after tax percentage (see below). It is calculated as follows:

$$\text{Operating profit percentage} = \frac{\text{Operating profit}}{\text{Sales}} \times 100$$

$$\text{MEL 2001 operating profit percentage} = \frac{25{,}385}{185{,}000} \times 100 = 13.72\%$$

$$\text{MEL 2000 operating profit percentage} = \frac{7{,}400}{160{,}000} \times 100 = 4.63\%$$

Comment on MEL

Operating profit percentage has improved quite dramatically from 4.63 per cent to 13.72 per cent (almost three times). While there have been no savings in operating costs (in fact they have gone up by £1,570), the improvement is due entirely to the extra volume of business – it has moved further ahead of break-even sales. This supports the old belief that, as a business moves past break-even, all the additional gross profit moves down to operating profit and net profit.

How do I improve it?

After you have improved GP per cent and increased sales, attack all the business operating costs (salaries, cars, stationery etc.). For more details on improving operating profit refer to FAQ 15.

3. Net profit after tax to sales (net profit after tax percentage)

The net profit after tax percentage expresses net profit after tax (PAT) as a percentage of sales. It shows how profitable a business is after all business costs (trading and financing) and after it has allowed for tax. It gives some measure of how much profit will be available for giving to the shareholders (dividends) and how much, if any, will be left for future growth and development of the business.

It is calculated as follows:

$$\text{Net profit after tax percentage} = \frac{\text{Net profit after tax}}{\text{Sales}} \times 100$$

$$\text{MEL 2001 net profit percentage} = \frac{18,665}{185,000} \times 100 = 10.09\%$$

$$\text{MEL 2000 net profit percentage} = \frac{4,050}{160,000} \times 100 = 2.53\%$$

Comment on MEL

Operating profit percentage has improved quite dramatically from 2.53 per cent to 10.09 per cent (almost four times). This shows that the further saving in bank interest has compounded the improvement at the operating-profit level.

How do I improve it?

After you have improved operating profit, attack your financing costs (hire purchase, development loans, bank loans etc.). For more details on reducing loan repayments refer to FAQ 15. Another course of action is to save tax, which can be done by making payments into pension funds, buying capital assets, etc.

Measures of profitability (external measures)

4. Return on capital employed (ROCE)

The return-on-capital-employed percentage (ROCE per cent) expresses operating profit (see 2 above) as a percentage of capital employed. It shows how much profit (or return) is available to all the providers of the long-term capital (shareholders and long-term creditors). If this return is high it indicates that the business will be able to attract additional funding if needed. Conversely, if it is low (below other similar investments), then the business will be unable to attract any additional funding.

Calculation of capital employed

Because of the modern format of the balance sheet, it is often quite difficult to identify the capital-employed figure. Capital employed can be measured in either of two ways – they both give the same figure:

a. Fixed assets + net current assets (current assets – current liabilities) + capital and reserves (share capital + reserves), or
b. Capital and reserves + long-term creditors (creditors due after 12 months).

It is calculated as follows:

$$\text{ROCE percentage} = \frac{\text{Operating profit}}{\text{(a) or (b) above}} \times 100$$

$$\text{MEL 2001 ROCE} = \frac{25{,}385}{28{,}910} \times 100 = 87.81\%$$

$$\text{MEL 2000 ROCE} = \frac{7{,}400}{24{,}500} \times 100 = 30.20\%$$

Comment on MEL

ROCE has improved quite dramatically from 30.20 per cent to 87.81 per cent (almost three times). This reflects the improvement in operating profit (see 2 above) on basically similar capital employed. This business would now be considered a very attractive proposition for further external funding.

How do I improve it?

If you have access to other free or cheaper funds, pay off the most expensive borrowing you have. Get rid of assets that the business does not need (or use efficiently) and convert these to cash.

5. Return on shareholders' capital (ROSC)

The return-on-shareholders'-capital percentage (ROSC per cent) expresses net profit after tax (see 3 above) as a percentage of shareholders' capital (capital and reserves). It shows how much profit (or return) is available to the shareholders (just one group of providers of the long-term capital). If this return is high it indicates that the business will be able to attract additional funding if needed. Conversely, if it is low (below bank base rate), then the business will be unable to attract any additional funding.

It is calculated as follows:

$$\text{ROSC percentage} = \frac{\text{Net profit after tax}}{\text{Capital and reserves}} \times 100$$

$$\text{MEL 2001 ROSC} = \frac{18,665}{18,910} \times 100 = 98.70\%$$

$$\text{MEL 2001 ROSC} = \frac{4,050}{245} \times 100 = 1653.06\%$$

Comment on MEL

ROSC looks to have dropped very dramatically from 1,653.06 per cent to 98.70 per cent. However, this ratio merits further investigation. ROSC has dropped because year 2000 was based on shareholders' capital almost wiped out by accumulated business losses. This has led the year 2000 ROSC figure to be overinflated. To avoid this sort of distortion you could use just the share capital value (£10,000), in which case the year 2000 figure would have been 40.5 per cent $\left(\frac{4,050}{10,000} \times 100 \right)$.

This would show a more than doubling of ROSC, which is nearer the mark.

How do I improve it?

After you have done everything else above, change the mix of equity to borrowings (gearing), which is shown below.

Manipulating borrowings to improve ROSC

In 5 and 6 above you have seen that there are two long-term methods of funding a business – equity (shareholders) and debt (borrowing long-term). By changing the mix of these two, or gearing, as it is known, it is possible to improve ROSC – assuming the business is both profitable and able to borrow the additional funds. The table below shows how this can work.

In this example a business needs £15,000 of capital and has £5,000 of operating profit. If it uses only share capital to fund the business (all equity or no gearing) then ROSC is 26.67 per cent. However, by using increasing amounts of long-term debt (gearing), the ROSC improves to 45.33 per cent (average or 50 per cent gearing) and finally to 64 per cent (high or 66.67 per cent gearing).

However, in deciding whether they will lend to a business,

financial institutions (banks) will consider the level of gearing and interest cover – ability to service the debt. These are covered in FAQ 31.

The effect of gearing on ROSC

	No gearing	Average gearing	High gearing
Share capital	15,000	7,500	5,000
Long-term debt	0	7,500	10,000
Total capital	15,000	15,000	15,000
Operating profit	5,000	5,000	5,000
Less loan interest (10%)	0	750	1,000
Net profit before tax	5,000	4,250	4,000
Less tax @ 20%	1,000	850	800
Net profit after tax	4,000	3,400	3,200

$$(1)\ ROSC\ =\ \dfrac{4,000}{15,000}\qquad \dfrac{3,400}{7,500}\qquad \dfrac{3,200}{5,000}$$

	No gearing	Average gearing	High gearing
	26.67%	45.33%	64.00%

Where can I get further help?

You should look at the following:

- Read the other FAQs on business control.
- Read *Business Accounting*, 1 and 2, by Frank Wood (Pitman Publishing, 1996).
- Contact your accountant.

FAQ 30

'How can I control my working capital?'

What do I need to know?

When we looked at return on capital employed (ROCE) in FAQ 29, we saw that the capital element comprised fixed assets + net current assets. As you may recall, fixed assets do not change very much on a day-to-day basis. However, net current assets, which we also call working capital, are constantly on the change (FAQ 3 shows this in the working-capital cycle). Hopefully, if you have read the FAQs on working capital and short-term funding (FAQs 1 to 9), you will already be convinced of the importance of working capital in both growth and mature businesses. It is important to monitor and control how the various elements of working capital (debtors, stock, trade creditors etc.) are moving in relation to sales (**efficiency**). For example, as sales grow, are debtors growing at the same rate (good) or faster (bad)? If any of these grow disproportionately, the business may run out of cash.

At the same time, the relationship between current assets and current liabilities needs to be monitored and controlled to see if the business can still meet its liabilities – i.e. pay its debts when required. We call this **liquidity**.

This FAQ looks specifically at measures of working capital (both efficiency and liquidity), and explains how to use them and what they mean. We shall be using Mark Engineering Ltd (MEL) (see Appendix) as an example for the calculation of these ratios. Each of the ratios has been calculated for the years 2001 and 2000 and given together with a brief commentary on any changes.

Measures of liquidity (ability to pay)

Common sense tells us that a business uses its current assets to meet its current liabilities. The following two ratios focus on a business's ability to pay its creditors.

1. Current ratio

The current ratio expresses current assets as a ratio to current liabilities. It is used to indicate whether there are sufficient short-term assets to meet the short-term liabilities. If a business cannot pay its creditors on time (see FAQ 7 on creditor strain) then it will find it very difficult to continue trading.

Unfortunately, there is no universally accepted 'norm' for the current ratio – it varies from sector to sector. While the hotel trade may find a current ratio of 0.25 : 1 (i.e., its current ratios are a quarter of its current liabilities) acceptable, a manufacturing business would find that totally unacceptable, requiring a current ratio of nearer 1.5 : 1 (i.e., its current ratios are 1¼ times its current liabilities) to be considered safe.

It is calculated as follows:

Current ratio = Current assets : current liabilities

MEL 2001 current ratio = 23,100 : 6,690 = 3.45 : 1

MEL 2000 current ratio = 17,050 : 15,050 = 1.13 : 1

Comment on MEL

Current ratio looks to have improved very dramatically from 1.13 to 3.45 (over three times). The business has certainly improved its ability to pay its liabilities. This is due to the improvement in net profit by £14,615 (£18,665 − £4,050), which has created higher debtors, higher stock holding, and additional cash, which has been used to clear overdraft.

How do I improve it?

Attack everything that improves profit (see FAQ 15). Speed up the conversion of stock into sales and the collection of debtors. This will improve the cash position and therefore the ability to pay creditors on time.

2. Acid test or quick ratio

This is a far more critical measure than the current ratio, because it excludes assets that cannot be converted into cash quickly, such as stock and work in progress. Again, there is no absolute 'norm', but many businesses do operate with acid-test ratios of less than 1 : 1 but appear to have no problem in paying their creditors on time.

It is calculated as follows:

Acid test = Current assets (excluding all stocks) : current liabilities

MEL 2001 acid test = 13,100 : 6,690 = 1.96 : 1

MEL 2000 acid test = 10,050 : 15,050 = 0.67 : 1

Comment on MEL

Acid test looks to have improved very dramatically from 0.67 to 1.96 (nearly three times). The business has certainly improved its ability to pay its liabilities. Explained in the same as 1 above.

How do I improve it?

Take the same action as per current ratio (see above).

Measures of efficiency

Common sense also tells us that if a business can improve the speed at which it converts stock into sales (stock turn) and collect its debtors (debtor days) and delay its creditor payments (creditor days) it will improves its cash position. The following three ratios focus on how efficiently a business deals with these three areas.

3. Stock turn

Stock turn measures how efficiently a business converts its stock into sales. This measure shows how many times a year stock is 'turned over' or sold – the higher this figure the better. The sole purpose of carrying stock is to sell it (as quickly as possible) for as much as possible (GP per cent). Therefore, the longer it remains unsold the more it costs in lost (or paid) bank interest and delayed profit.

It is calculated as follows:

$$\text{Stock turn} = \frac{\text{Cost of sales}}{\text{All stocks}} \text{ times a year}$$

$$\text{MEL 2001 stock turn} = \frac{79,945}{10,000} = 7.99 \text{ times a year}$$

$$\text{MEL 2000 stock turn} = \frac{74,500}{7,000} = 10.64 \text{ times a year}$$

Comment on MEL

Stock turn has got worse, down from 10.64 times a year to 7.99 times. Clearly the business is 'stocking up' to meet higher sales, but has done so disproportionately. However, a 40 per cent increase in stocks to meet a 15.63 per cent growth in sales (see FAQ 36)? Stock purchasing is out of control.

How do I improve it?

Attack everything that affects stock holding (e.g., production, buying). See FAQ 15 for more detail on how to cut down stock days.

Note: Stock turn can also be calculated as stock days (i.e. the number of days goods are held in stock). In this case the lower the number of days the better.

It is calculated as follows:

$$\text{Stock days} = \frac{\text{All stocks}}{\text{Cost of sales}} \times 365 \text{ days}$$

$$\text{MEL 2001 stock days} = \frac{10,000}{79,945} \times 365 = 45.66 \text{ days}$$

$$\text{MEL 2000 stock days} = \frac{7,000}{74,500} \times 365 = 34.29 \text{ days}$$

4. Debtor days

Debtor days measures how efficiently a business collects the money due to it from its customers (debtors). This measure shows on average how many days it takes to collect your outstanding debts. A figure of, say, 60 days says that it is taking nearly two months on average to collect your money (see FAQ 6 for a very accurate way to calculate debtor days). The higher this figure, the more inefficient is your debtor collection process.

It is calculated as follows:

$$\text{Debtor days} = \frac{\text{Debtors}}{\text{Sales}} \times 365 \text{ days}$$

$$\text{MEL 2001 debtor days} = \frac{13,000}{185,000} \times 365 = 25.65 \text{ days}$$

$$\text{MEL 2000 debtor days} = \frac{10,000}{160,000} \times 365 = 22.81 \text{ days}$$

Comment on MEL

The debtor-days figure has got worse, up from 22.81 days to 25.65 days. This means that it is taking nearly three days longer to collect debts. While this may not seem very significant in itself, if the business continues to grow and debtor collection continues to increase, the overall working capital requirement (debtors + stock) will increase. Needs tightening up.

How do I improve it?

Attack everything in the debtor process from invoicing to collection. See FAQ 15 for more detail on how to cut down debtor days.

5. Creditor days

Of course the final piece in the jigsaw is the time it takes a business to pay its suppliers (creditors). Ideally if, in our example, it takes the business nearly 26 days to be paid by its customers it should be paying its suppliers in, say, 30-plus days. That way it is not being 'squeezed' and having to pay its suppliers before it gets its money in. Creditor days measures how well a business is managing its supplier payments.

A word of warning: do not think that taking 60–90 days to pay your suppliers is good cash management. If you take this long you will really hack off your suppliers with consequent dire results (see FAQ 7 on creditor strain).

It is calculated as follows:

$$\text{Creditor days} = \frac{\text{Creditors}}{\text{Cost of sales}} \times 365 \text{ days}$$

$$\text{MEL 2001 creditor days} = \frac{1,690}{79,945} \times 365 = 7.72 \text{ days}$$

$$\text{MEL 2000 creditor days} = \frac{2,000}{74,500} \times 365 = 9.80 \text{ days}$$

Comment on MEL

The creditor-days figure has got shorter, from 9.8 days to 7.72 days. This means that the business is paying its suppliers just over two days earlier. On its own this is not a problem, but taking into account the slight worsening of debtor collection (debtor days) and stock control (stock turn), the overall working capital position is getting worse (see 6 below).

How do I improve it?

Paying suppliers features very low down in the list of most business priorities. However, if you can pay suppliers early or at least on time you do get loyalty from them. I have two particular clients who pay me within days of receipt of my invoice – they always get prompt service from me and priority over other clients if I am busy. Who says money doesn't talk? It screams! However, you can pay your suppliers only if you have got cash – so you will need to work on debtors, stocks etc.

Some 'broader' indicators of working-capital efficiency and fixed assets

While we are still on the subject of efficiency, there are two more ratios that are worthy of mention. Unlike the others that we have outlined that focus on specific areas (e.g., debtors, stock), these ratios reflect the overall efficiency of working-capital management and fixed-asset management.

6. Circulation of working capital

Circulation of working capital measures how efficiently working capital (net current assets) is being used to support the sales of the business. The greater the number of times working capital is being turned the better. Its main use is in planning and monitoring working-capital requirements. For example, if a business can support £10 of sales with each £1 of working capital and it is planning to grow its sales from £1 million to £2 million, then it will have to find another £100,000 of working capital $\dfrac{(£1,000,000)}{£10}$

Assuming it can get some additional trade credit, the remainder of the additional £100,000 cash (working capital) will have to come from outside sources.

It is calculated as follows:

$$\text{Circulation of working capital} = \frac{\text{Sales}}{\text{Net current assets}} \text{ times}$$

$$\text{MEL 2001 circulation of working capital} = \frac{185,000}{16,410} = 11.27 \text{ times}$$

$$\text{MEL 2000 circulation of working capital} = \frac{160,000}{2,000} = 80.00 \text{ times}$$

Comment on MEL

At first glance it looks as if working capital is being used less efficiently – it has gone down from 80 times to 11.27 times. However, this is more a comment on the amount of working capital the business had in year 2000, which was particularly low – the low values for current ratio and acid test tend to confirm this. Consequently, a comparison between 2001 and 2000 is very difficult. It may make more sense to compare the 2000 circulation-of-working-capital figure to that of a competitor to see if it is good (or not).

How do I improve it?

The objective is to grow sales while maintaining net current assets at a similar or slightly lower percentage. This means better stock control (to turn stock over faster) and better debtor collection (to improve cash), while at the same time stretching creditors (but not past the point of creditor strain). Any surplus cash not needed as working capital should be reinvested in the business to drive up sales and profitability.

7. Asset turn

Asset turn measures how many pounds in sales each pound of fixed assets generates. Its purpose is to show how efficiently a business is using its fixed assets. The principle is that the higher the value of sales that each fixed asset is generating the better. You may have heard the expression 'sweating your assets'. This is what it means. In calculating this ratio I would suggest that you include only tangible assets.

It is calculated as follows:

$$\text{Asset turn} = \frac{\text{Sales}}{\text{Fixed assets @ NBV}}$$

$$\text{MEL 2001 asset turn} = \frac{185,000}{12,500} = \pounds 14.80$$

$$\text{MEL 2000 asset turn} = \frac{160,000}{22,500} = \pounds 7.11$$

Comment on MEL

There has been an improvement in the used of fixed assets – each pound's worth is now supporting £14.80 of sales compared with £7.11 (just over two times as much). This indicates a more efficient use of fixed assets. However, if we look more closely it is apparent that the aggressive depreciation during 2001 has reduced net book value (NBV) disproportionately, leading to an apparent better performance during 2001. My suggestion would be that instead of NBV you use original cost (if available). Unfortunately, we do not have this information in this example. An improvement in asset turn could be used as a justification to make additional investment in fixed assets, or if this figure was low it might be used as an excuse to deny the funding of more fixed assets.

How do I improve it?

The business should constantly be reviewing its use of fixed assets. If there are motor vehicles check if they are fully utilised – check business mileage. Dispose of any unnecessary assets. As sales grow don't rush to buy additional fixed assets. If you need to make further investment see if you can buy used equipment to save cost (and so boost asset turn).

<u>Where can I get further help?</u>

You should look at the following:

- Read the other FAQs on business control.
- Read *Business Accounting*, 1 and 2, by Frank Wood (Pitman Publishing, 1996).
- Contact your accountant.

FAQ 31

'How can I make sure that my business is still growing and that I am not taking undue risk?'

What do I need to know?

How do you know if your business is growing? The most obvious measures must be those that highlight sales and profit growth over recent years. However, there are other aspects of growth that are just as important – those that measure the growth delivered by your workforce. With many businesses finding recruiting and retaining skilled personnel a real problem, it makes sense to get the most out of those that you already have.

A businessman I spoke with recently quite openly said that he would not employ anyone who would not add value – and his yardstick was the average added value per employee. If, for example, his average added value per employee was £80,000 then any new employees would be expected to exceed this. In the case of a salesperson, this is, of course, relatively easy to measure. However, you may wonder how you would measure this for, say, an administrator. His view was that and support staff would be measured on the front-line improvement they would bring. For example, if their employment would enable other salespeople to improve their added value by £80,000 collectively, then that person was meeting the required target.

Another concern that you may have as your business grows is that of financial risk. Does it have the right mix of debt and equity funding (this is referred to as gearing)? Businesses that have a much higher proportion of debt than equity are referred to as highly geared. This is particularly relevant, because debt has a cost (interest and capital) that must be paid on time and in full regardless of the profitability of the business. When times are hard (e.g., during a recession) businesses that are highly geared are usually the first to go bust.

Of course, gearing is just one measure of financial risk. Another, which should be used in conjunction with gearing, is interest cover. Interest cover measures a business's ability to service its debt. In a way it's a bit like when you go to a bank or building society to borrow money to buy a property. They look at how easily you can cover the mortgage payments and will give you a mortgage of only four or five times your salary.

This FAQ looks specifically at measures of growth and risk and explains how to use them and what they mean. We shall be using Mark Engineering Ltd (MEL) (see Appendix) as an example for the calculation of these ratios. Each of the ratios has been calculated for the years 2001 and 2000 and is given with a brief commentary on any changes.

1. Sales growth

This shows year-on-year growth in sales, expressed as a percentage. It's used to show whether your business has grown over the last twelve months and by how much.

It is calculated as follows:

$$\text{Sales growth percentage} = \frac{\text{This year's sales} - \text{last year's sales}}{\text{Last year's sales}} \times 100$$

$$\text{MEL 2001 sales growth} = \frac{(185,000 - 160,000)}{160,000} \times 100 = 15.63\%$$

$$\text{MEL 2000 sales growth} = \text{Not available}$$

Comment on MEL

Unfortunately we do not have sufficient information to calculate sales growth for 2000 (we would need 1999 sales for this calculation). However, sales growth has been 15.63 per cent, which at first sight looks quite good – unless of course this is less than last year or less than a competitor.

How do I improve it?

Sell more (easier said than done).

2. Profit growth

This shows year-on-year growth in net profit after tax (PAT), expressed as a percentage. It is used to show how 'bottom line' profit is being maintained against sales over the last twelve months.

It is calculated as follows:

$$\text{Profit after growth percentage} = \frac{\text{This year's PAT} - \text{last year's PAT}}{\text{Last year's PAT}} \times 100$$

$$\text{MEL 2001 profit growth} = \frac{(18,665 - 4,050)}{4,050} \times 100 = 360.86\%$$

$$\text{MEL 2000 profit growth} = \text{Not available}$$

Comment on MEL

Sales have grown by a phenomenal 360.86 per cent (over three times) in the last twelve months. This has happened as a result of all the other things we have seen earlier (e.g., sales growth, improvement in gross profit percentage).

How do I improve it?

Increase sales, improve gross profit and reduce operating and financing costs.

3. Sales per employee

Shows improvement in sales revenue generated by each employee. This is just one of three measures that can be used to measure the growth (or otherwise) in the effective use of the employees of a business. Can be used as a justification for employing more staff (e.g., if it can be shown that the current sales-per-employee figure is close to capacity for a certain group of employees, such as salespeople, then further growth in 1 and 2 above may be restricted if additional salespeople are not recruited). Conversely, it can be used to reduce staff levels if the figure is very low.

It is calculated as follows:

$$\text{Sales per employee } (£) = \frac{£\,\text{Sales}}{\text{Number of employees}}$$

$$\text{MEL 2001 sales per employee} = \frac{£185,000}{5} = £37,000$$

$$\text{MEL 2000 sales per employee} = \frac{£160,000}{4} = £40,000$$

Comment on MEL

The figures show that sales per employee have fallen from £40,000 to £37,000. Sales have grown but there does not appear to have been full benefit from the extra employee. The business needs to continue to monitor this and if the necessary sales improvement does not follow perhaps look to put that person on part-time work or replace them – if it proves they are not effective.

How do I improve it?
Increase sales without taking on any more employees, or cut employee numbers.

4. Profit per employee
Similar measure to 3, showing how profitably people have been employed in the business after the full business costs. Probably not as useful as sales per employee in measuring pure people performance, since most of the business costs are not people-related. However, this measure can be used to evaluate how much profit each person helps to create after the full business costs.

It is calculated as follows:

$$\text{Profit per employee } (£) = \frac{£ \text{ Net profit after tax (PAT)}}{\text{Number of employees}}$$

$$\text{MEL 2001 profit per employee} = \frac{£18,665}{5} = £3,733$$

$$\text{MEL 2001 profit per employee} = \frac{£4,050}{4} = £1,012$$

Comment on MEL
The figures show that profit per employee has increased from £1,012 to £3,733 (about 3.5 times). This has happened because the business is now accelerating past marginal profitability (in 2000) to good profitability (in 2001) at a rate higher than the take-on of employees. This is due to the predominantly fixed costs now being covered and all additional gross profit becoming net profit.

How do I improve it?
This is more a profit-improvement problem than a people-numbers problem, especially if sales per employee are static or have improved. See FAQ 15 for profit improvement ideas.

5. Value added per employee (VAPE)
Similar measure to 4 and 5, showing how much 'gross contribution' each employee has made. In effect it shows how much 'real' income

they have brought in (gross profit) to cover their remuneration and contribute to profit. Used to highlight the efficiency in the use of people in the business, especially if related to average remuneration.

It is calculated as follows:

$$\text{VAPE } (£) = \frac{£\text{ Sales} - (\text{materials} + \text{bought-in services in cost of sales})}{\text{Number of employees}}$$

$$\text{MEL 2001 VAPE} = \frac{£185,000 - (27,000 + 8,865)}{5} = £29,827$$

$$\text{MEL 2000 VAPE} = \frac{£160,000 - (24,000 + 8,500)}{5} = £25,500$$

Comment on MEL

Added value per employee has improved from £25,500 to £29,827. This is as a result of all the profit improvements we have seen earlier achieved at a faster rate than employee growth. However, how does this look if we take average employee remuneration into account? In 2001 average remuneration was

$$£17,024 \frac{(44,080 + 38,570 + 2,500)}{5}$$

and in 2000 it was $£20,625 \dfrac{(42,000 + 38,000 + 2,500)}{4}$

This shows that in 2001 the net contribution per employee was £12,803 (£29,827 − £17,024) compared with a 2000 figure of £4,875 (£25,500 − £20,625). This has shown a more dramatic increase − brought about by lower average remuneration (particularly in production wages)

How do I improve it?

Keep employee numbers to a minimum and invest in more capital equipment to help efficiency. As long as depreciation is lower than the remuneration it replaces, then this will improve added value.

6. Gearing

This measures how much of the long-term capital in the business has been provided by means of debt and is expressed as a percentage (e.g., 20 per cent). Borrowed money (debt) is regarded as risk money because it must be repaid (with interest) even if the business is loss-making – this being part of the risk a business takes when it takes it on. Gearing below 50 per cent is preferable to show that the business is not too dependent on borrowed money. This also leaves further scope for borrowing if the business needs it later.

Note: make sure to net off cash at bank against bank overdraft. If this results in a net cash-at-bank position take this off both the creditors' figures in the equation below.

It is calculated as follows:

$$\text{Gearing percentage} = \frac{\text{creditors (due after 12 months)} + \text{bank overdraft}}{\text{shareholders' funds} + \text{creditors} \text{ (due after 12 months)} + \text{bank overdraft}} \times 100$$

$$\text{MEL 2001 gearing} = \frac{10,000 + 5,000}{18,910 + 24,255 + 13,050} \times 100 = 26.68\%$$

$$\text{MEL 2000 gearing} = \frac{24,255 + 13,050}{245 + 24,255 + 13,050} \times 100 = 99.35\%$$

Comment on MEL

There has been a dramatic improvement in gearing from 99.35 per cent in 2000 to 26.68 per cent in 2001. The cause of the high gearing in 2000 was the cumulative losses having almost wiped out shareholders' funds while borrowing had risen to keep the business supplied with cash. In reality, it could only have been a very sympathetic bank manager who had allowed further borrowings when gearing reached such a high figure. The improvement in 2001 has come entirely from the business returning to good profitability and using the resulting cash to clear loans and overdraft. The business now has control over its funding – debt is now very manageable (see interest cover below for further comments).

How do I improve it?

A desperate business will try to get cash from any source if it is unprofitable. However, the common-sense approach is to deny further borrowings to these businesses. Any further cash should come from either existing shareholders or new shareholders – because they are in the business of providing risk money. Hopefully, with the fresh equity-cash investment, the business buys time to return to profitability. Any profits should be retained within the business (no dividends) so that cash flow is improved and gearing ultimately brought back to manageable levels.

7. Interest cover

This measures the ability of the business to meet the interest payments out of profit, expressed as number (e.g., five times). This measure should be used in conjunction with gearing (see 6 above) to provide an overall assessment of the risk. For example, there were many businesses that were founded almost entirely on borrowed money during the early 1980s, which technically were 100 per cent geared. However, during the boom period they were very profitable and could easily pay the interest charges. The problem arose when the recession came along and these businesses ceased being profitable. The high interest charges could not be covered by profit and so many of these businesses went bust.

It is calculated as follows:

$$\text{Interest cover} = \frac{\text{Operating profit}}{\text{Bank and loan interest}} \text{ times}$$

$$\text{MEL 2001 interest cover} = \frac{25,385}{500} = 50.77 \text{ times}$$

$$\text{MEL 2001 interest cover} = \frac{7,400}{2,000} = 3.7 \text{ times}$$

Comment on MEL

There has been a dramatic improvement in interest cover from 3.7 times to 50.77 times. The improvement has been brought about by the improved profit converting to cash and being used to clear of debt. As a result this has reduced interest charges. However, looking at 2000, where the gearing was over 90 per cent, the business was still able to meet its interest payments – but, had profits fallen slightly, then it would not have been able to. It was in quite a risky situation in 2000. Overall in 2001 it is in a very comfortable position – it can borrow more without gearing and interest cover becoming critical.

Where can I get further help?

You should look at the following:

> ■ Read the other FAQs on business control.
> ■ Read *Business Accounting*, 1 and 2, by Frank Wood (Pitman Publishing, 1996).
> ■ Contact your accountant.

FAQ 32

'What are the key numbers that I need to know to control my business?'

What do I need to know?

If you have looked at FAQs 28 to 31 you will have seen a whole 'menu' of ratios that can be used to monitor and control most aspects of a business. The problem is that if you calculated all of these each month it would be time-consuming and you might be doing more than you need. However, you cannot afford to ignore any of the areas covered by these ratios – unless they are completely irrelevant to your particular business. For example, if your business deals only in cash (e.g., a fish-and-chip shop) then you don't have a debtor problem and debtor days will be a worthless calculation.

The previous FAQs have identified going on for 20 ratios, which are probably relevant to most businesses some of the time. My suggestion would be that you have a regime of using all these ratios some of the time and a handful all of the time. So, for example, you should calculate all the ratios every quarter and the key ones every month. The next question then is: How do you identify the key numbers to control your business, those that you use more frequently? The key rules are:

> ■ What do you need to know to run your type of business (your business sector, e.g., retail, manufacturing, service etc.)?
> ■ What do you need to know specific to your business situation (e.g., growth, recovery, cash flow crisis)?

This FAQ sets out a framework for you to use to establish the key numbers to help you control your business.

Your business sector

Each business sector has its own characteristics, which will determine the key areas to monitor. To use a sporting analogy, it would not make any sense to coach a football team down at the nets with a bat, cricket ball and pads. These would be quite the wrong tools and techniques to apply to football coaching.

Retail

If you are a retailer, then you have quite specific issues. Typically, these are businesses that sell a large range of products, with different margins, in differing volumes. The businesses have one limiting factor, space, which cannot easily be increased. The other limiting factor, which usually can be addressed, is staff. Apart from these specifics they have the other normal business issues – profit, cash flow, funding etc.

In a typical retail business, then, the sector specific areas are:

> - **Stock** – ensuring that sufficient (but not too much) is held for anticipated sales; ensuring that slow-moving items are quickly identified so action can be taken.
> - **Product profitability** – ensuring that you know which products sell well, their average margins and the overall contribution to profit (related to the display space they occupy).
> - **Average customer spend** – the constant battle is to get customers to spend more, especially if there is little scope to increase the customer base. You need to know frequency of visit and average spend.
> - **Sales space** – if this is a limiting factor then it should be maximised and profit per square foot of display area monitored.
> - **Queue time/length** – customers do not like waiting and if they perceive the queue to be too long they will just dump their basket and shop elsewhere.

Armed with this knowledge, you should choose those ratios and the other financial and non-financial information that enable you to control these areas. My suggestion would be something like this:

> - **Stock**: use stock turn to give you a general 'health check' on overall stock. Then, either using a computerised stock system or stock cards, identify slow-moving stock and stock levels (measured in days' sales) to take specific action.

■ **Product profitability**: this is ideally suited to a computerised accounting system that incorporates stock control. Use this to run off a monthly (and year-to-date) report showing the following for each product: sales, cost of sales, average GP per cent, total contribution (sales revenue less cost of sales). This report should be run off in descending order of total contribution (i.e. showing all the big earners first and the small earners last). If you can superimpose on this the square-foot display area that each takes up you can work out contribution per square foot for each product – to see which are best utilising your limited display area.

■ **Average customer spend**: this information is best provided by electronic point-of-sale (EPOS) systems, such as electronic tills. These can produce this analysis for any period you want (e.g., hourly, daily, weekly). They can also show it for each till and compare one period with another (e.g., this week with last week, same time last year). For larger retailers, loyalty cards are used to track consumer spend and target them for special offers to persuade them to increase their spend.

■ **Sales space**: if a shop is already selling well it makes sense to make more sales space available. You should monitor how much sales space is available from month to month to make sure effective sales area is not diminishing. Look at imaginative ways to increase space available to sell from. Combine this with product profitability information to give floor space only to those products that meet your profit generation criteria. Regular restocking of shelves can increase sales area by ensuring that only small quantities are held on the sales floor – bulk stocks are kept in the stockroom.

■ **Queue time/length**: this has to be monitored visually, although EPOS systems can provide timed reading for each customer. This can be used to highlight operatives who may be slow and therefore causing queuing.

This is just a brief selection of the key information a retailer should be monitoring on a frequent basis.

Manufacturing

A different set of issues concerns a manufacturer. The key areas are related to manufacturing efficiency. If a business has several different production lines or machines, then throughput and cost for each are important.

With a typical manufacturer, then, the sector specific areas are:

- **Machine output** – ensuring that downtime is minimised and that throughput of good-quality product is high as possible.
- **Material costs** – ensuring that wastage is minimised and that maximum product is used at minimum material cost.
- **Labour cost** – ensuring that maximum production is achieved for lowest labour cost.
- **Order-to-sale time** – ensuring that work is progressed through the system as quickly as possible to speed up profit generation and minimise cash tied up in raw materials, work in progress and finished goods.
- **Stock** – ensuring that sufficient (but not too much) is held for anticipated sales; ensuring that slow-moving items are quickly identified so action can be taken.
- **Product recall/rectification** – to ensure this is minimised.

Armed with this knowledge, you should choose those ratios and the other financial and non-financial information that enable you to control these areas. My suggestion would be something like this:

- **Machine output**: measure hours worked, downtime, rejects, sales revenue and gross profit generated per hour/job/shift/day/week/month etc. for each machine/production line and compare with previous periods to observe trends.
- **Material costs**: measure material costs as a percentage of sales for each job for each machine/production line and compare with previous periods to observe trends.
- **Labour cost**: measure labour costs as a percentage of sales for each hour/job/shift/day/week/month etc. for each machine/production line and compare with previous periods to observe trends.
- **Order-to-sale time**: track all jobs from start to finish noting times for each key stage.
- **Stock**: use stock turn to give you a general 'health check' on overall stock. Then, either using a computerised stock system or stock cards, identify slow moving stock and stock levels (measured in days' sales) to take specific action.
- **Product recall/rectification**: record all instances by product with cost and relate to total sales of product to see if per cent is increasing. Trace back to operative/machine/shift etc. to take corrective action and anticipate further recall/rectification.

This is just a brief selection of the key information a manufacturer should be monitoring on a frequent basis.

Service

A different set of issues concerns a service provider. The key areas are related to service delivery. This is people- and time-related. In general, there is very little stock, although in some cases parts will be an element of the service provided (e.g., repair parts, service upgrades).

In a typical service, then, the sector-specific areas are:

> ■ **Service calls** – ensuring that the target number of calls are made, that arrival is on time, calls completed within time, and do not require return visits.
>
> ■ **Service cost** – ensuring that labour and material costs are kept under control.
>
> ■ Service profit – ensuring that each person responsible for delivering the service is delivering maximum profit.
>
> ■ **Service scheduling/control** – ensuring that service engineers/jobs are scheduled to maximise profitability.

Armed with this knowledge, you should choose those ratios and the other financial and non-financial information that enables you to control these areas. My suggestion would be something like this:

> ■ **Service calls**: all engineers should produce visit reports so that the number of calls made in a day/week/month can be monitored. Also, these will give call lengths so that job/customer profitability can be measured and monitored. All customers/contracts should have cost records on which service time is entered (as well as other costs and revenues) to monitor profitability.
>
> ■ **Service cost**: a record should be kept of business mileage and vehicle costs (petrol, repairs, insurance etc.) for all external service providers. Labour costs for both internal and external service providers should be recorded and monitored daily/weekly/monthly for each customer/job type.
>
> ■ **Service profit**: a record should be kept for each service engineer/service provider to monitor their profitability. This would combine service costs and service revenues and be analysed by person/customer/job type on a daily/weekly/monthly basis.

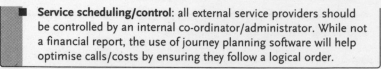

■ **Service scheduling/control**: all external service providers should be controlled by an internal co-ordinator/administrator. While not a financial report, the use of journey planning software will help optimise calls/costs by ensuring they follow a logical order.

This is just a brief selection of the key information a manufacturer should be monitoring on a frequent basis.

Your business situation

The second perspective to put on deciding what financial information a business needs to monitor relates entirely to its business situation. To use another sporting analogy, if a team is having a difficult time (e.g., it's on a bit of a losing streak), then, regardless of the type of sport, a motivational expert could be called in. The skills that they can bring will not be specific to any one sport but will be helpful for the current situation – moving from losing to winning.

So it is with the business – you need to know what the current pressing business situation is. Only then will you know what financial information you really need to monitor and control the current situation. Outlined below are the main business situations that you may encounter:

■ Start-up and early growth – the need is for cash sufficiency, budgetary control and meeting sales-growth targets.

■ Fast growth – the need is for cash sufficiency and maintaining growth and profitability.

■ Maturity – shareholder return, profit maintenance, protecting what the business has achieved.

■ Recovery – profit improvement, cash flow management and borrowing management.

■ Disposal/sale – profit optimisation, stability.

With these in mind, my shopping list of essential financial information would be like this:

Start-up and early growth
   a. Break-even point
   b. Cash flow management – debtor days, creditor days, stock turn
   c. Profitability – GP per cent, operating profit percentage, net profit percentage

    d. Growth – sales growth percentage, value added per employee

    e. Risk – gearing, interest cover

Fast growth

    a. Break-even profit point

    b. Cash flow management – debtor days, creditor days, stock turn, acid test

    c. Profitability – GP per cent, operating profit percentage, net profit percentage

    d. Risk – gearing, interest cover

Maturity

    a. Return on shareholders' capital (ROSC)

    b. Net profit percentage

    c. Current ratio

    d. Cash flow management – debtor days, creditor days, stock turn, acid test

Recovery

    a. Break-even point

    b. Profitability – GP per cent, operating profit percentage, net profit percentage

    c. Cash flow management – debtor days, creditor days, stock turn

    d. Risk – gearing, interest cover

Disposal/sale

    a. Profitability – GP per cent, operating profit percentage, net profit percentage

    b. Return on capital employed (ROCE)

    c. Growth – sales growth

These are the 'generic' monitoring tools that businesses should be using as a minimum. On top of these would be the industry-specific measures, which will tend to be more operational – these would have been identified under the 'your business sector' analysis.

Where can I get further help?

You should look at the following:

> ■ Read the other FAQs on business control.
> ■ Read *Business Accounting*, 1 and 2, by Frank Wood (Pitman Publishing, 1996).
> ■ Contact your accountant.

FAQ 33

'How do I justify spending any money at all on capital projects that will improve my business?'

What do I need to know?

No businesses voluntarily spend money on capital projects, such as plant and machinery, motor vehicles and office equipment. They do so for one of two main reasons:

1. Lack of capacity/improve efficiency (current problem)

There is a current restriction in the business, which, if nothing is done to remove it, will lead to lost business, reduced profitability and possible collapse of the business. A good example of this would be where a business has equipment that is already working at maximum capacity and due to the volume of orders has a large (and possibly increasing) backlog of work. This is denying the business the ability to do this work (and earn the profit) as quickly as it should. It is also running the risk of losing some of the customers because of the poor service it is offering.

2. New business potential (future opportunity)

The business has one or more new business opportunities that can deliver measurable revenues but will require capital (and possible revenue) expenditure. The difficulty may lie in choosing which opportunity to take on when each has different costs and benefits.

As a further complication capital projects usually span several years from start to either profitability or completion. The key criteria that will influence the decision-making process are:

> ■ Investment required – because the business will have limited funds
> ■ Return – because the business will want to maximise the rate of return

Time scale – because the business wants to make profit sooner rather than later

This FAQ looks at ways of evaluating capital projects to make sure that those that best meet the criteria above are chosen.

Method 1: Average rate of return (ARR)

By far and away the simplest way of evaluating a capital project is to measure the average profit it generates over its life and express this as an average – average rate of return (ARR). Once again, an example will show us how this works.

A business is considering buying a piece of equipment, which will have a one-off cost of £6,000. It will have a working life of five years, after which it will have no value. The table below shows the net profits (after full depreciation).

ARR example

Year	Option 1 Net profit
1	500
2	1,000
3	3,000
4	4,000
5	500
Total 5 years	9,000

On this project the average return over five years is £1,800 (£9,000/5 years). And since the investment is £6,000 the ARR is 30 per cent (£1,800/£6,000). This can then be compared with other projects being considered – to see which offers the highest ARR. Also, it can be measured against any minimum level of return that the business may set – e.g., it may stipulate that all projects must at least match the current ROCE rate being achieved by the business.

Limitations of ARR

Timing differences

Beautifully simple though the ARR method may be, it does have some limitations – it does not recognise timing differences. Two capital projects that yield the same average return but in different years (one in the early years and one in the later years) would both be evaluated as equal under the ARR method. It would not recognise that receiving profits earlier is better than later. The table below shows how this might occur.

Year	Option 1 Net profit	Option 2 Net profit
1	500	3,000
2	1,000	3,000
3	3,000	2,000
4	4,000	500
5	500	500
Total 5 years	9,000	9,000

Using ARR, these two projects would be treated as identical. However, we can see that Option 2 brings in profit earlier than Option 1. In fact we can see that by the end of the second year Option 2 has paid for itself (£6,000 cumulative profits = £6,000 investment). By comparison it is not until partway through Year 4 that the business has made the same level of cumulative profit.

ARR does not recognise that the capital project that has an earlier payback is more attractive.

Profit versus cash flow

ARR, as you will have noticed, measures profit on investment. Two projects may yield identical profits but, if one generated those profits in immediate cash, then ARR would not recognise this. Common sense, however, tells us that you would choose the project that brought in the cash soonest.

ARR does not recognise that a project that brings in cash more quickly is more attractive.

Overall, we would have to say that ARR is useful only if just one project is up for consideration. However, it is the starting point for most project evaluation.

Method 2: Payback period

This approach, already referred to, has become the most popular method for evaluating capital projects. Payback tries to overcome the two limitations of ARR. It compares the initial cash cost of the investment with the subsequent cash inflows. This recognition that cash rather than profit should be the measure is the important difference between payback and ARR. Payback also deals with the timing issue by measuring the time taken for the initial cost to be recovered. Once again an example will show us how this works.

A business is considering buying a piece of equipment that will have a one-off cost of £6,000. It will have a working life of five years, after which it will have no value. The table below shows the net cash flows.

Payback example	
	£
Initial project cost	6,000
Net cash inflows	
Year	
1	1,000
2	2,000
3	3,000
4	2,000
5	500

The payback period is three years. This is when the initial cost (£6,000) will have been covered by the annual net cash flows of Year 1 (£1,000), Year 2 (£2,000) and Year 3 (£3,000).

Now we have a method that uses cash and takes into account time. Of course this method does not tell us what return the business will make – you will have to use ARR as well to calculate this.

Limitations of payback period

While payback does take into account the timing of cash flows – the earlier they come the quicker the payback – it ignores all subsequent cash flows. It therefore is incapable of showing which of more than one option is better if both have the same payback period. Once again, an example will show us how this works. A business is considering two projects with the initial investments and net cash inflows shown in the table below.

	Option 1	Option 2
Initial project cost	6,000	6,000
Net cash inflows		
Year		
1	1,000	2,000
2	2,000	2,000
3	3,000	2,000
4	2,000	2,000
5	500	2,000
Total cash inflow	8,500	10,000
Payback period	3 years	3 years

As far as payback is concerned both options are equally attractive. However, common sense tells us that Option 2 must have the edge because it provides an additional £1,500 cash during its lifetime.

On its own, payback is not a good method for evaluating capital projects. It is capable of telling you only which projects will meet a predetermined cut of criteria (e.g., a business will accept only those projects that have a payback of less than x years. Payback should be used in conjunction with other capital project evaluation methods.

Method 3: Discounted cash flow (DCF)

In the previous two methods it has been noted that the timing of cash or profit flow is important. In a project where cash flows may come in over five or more years, we have assumed that a pound in five years' time has the same value as a pound today. This is not so. No one would willingly swap £1 today for £1 in five years' time. They would need compensating for the loss of value in the £1 over the five years. The exact amount of compensation required may be open to some debate, but it would be akin to something that equated to an investment with similar levels of risk. One might argue that a risk-free investment might carry a 6 per cent rate, whereas a high-risk investment something nearer to 20 per cent.

Using this same principle, discounted cash flow (DCF) attempts to convert cash flows from several different years into cash flows of common value. It does this by applying an agreed present-value factor (PVF) to the cash flows in each year to discount them back to a net present value (NPV) – i.e. today's value. While you can work out the present-value factors there are tables published for the various percentages and years that you may want to use (see APPENDIX for some PVF tables).

Once again, an example will show us how this works. The table below shows the net cash flows for a project under consideration. At the start (Year 0) the capital cost is £6,000, which is shown as –6,000 (because it is cash going out). Thereafter, from Year 1 through to Year 6, each year shows £2,000 coming in. Over the course of the five years the net cash flow is £4,000, which shows that the project more than covers its costs.

However, the business has set a target return for its investments of 20 per cent – so it has used this as its discount factor. As a result the investment stops looking so attractive. In fact, over five years, the net present value (NPV) of the cash flows has been reduced quite dramatically. Overall the NPV is –£424, which means it does not quite cover all the costs.

Year	Net cash flows	PVF 20%	NPV
0	–6,000	1	–6,000
1	750	0.833333	625
2	1,250	0.694444	868
3	4,000	0.578704	2,315
4	2,000	0.482253	965
5	2,000	0.401878	804
	4,000		–424

Using DCF we would reject this project because it does not show a positive NPV. The timing of cash flow over the life of a project is critical and this must be taken into account in the decision-making process. It is interesting to note that, when we use payback, we see that this project has a payback period of exactly three years, which probably would have been acceptable. Also, using, ARR it would have achieved a satisfactory 33.33 per cent.

DCF is a superior method of evaluating capital projects that have cash flows over many years because it recognises the time value of money.

Limitation of DCF

By now you must be thinking that none of the three methods is perfect – and you are nearly right. The only real limitation of DCF is that it would not be able to differentiate between two projects that had identical net present values but had different capital investment values. Fortunately, we can use DCF under these circumstances by constructing a profitability index.

Profitability index (PI)

The profitability index takes DCF a stage further by providing a comparison between projects that have identical NPVs – a sort of 'tie breaker'. Once again, an example will show us how this works.

Project 1 and Project 2 require initial capital investments of £6,000 and £12,000 respectively. They have identical NPVs of £365, which means they both meet the business's 15 per cent return target.

	Project 1 Net cash flows	PVF 15%	NPV	Project 2 Net cash flows	PVF 15%	NPV
Year	£		£	£		£
0	−6,000	1	−6,000	−12,000	1	−12,000
1	750	0.869565	652	1,500	0.869565	1,304
2	1,250	0.756144	945	2,500	0.756144	1,890
3	4,000	0.657516	2,630	8,000	0.657516	5,260
4	2,000	0.571753	1,144	4,000	0.571753	2,287
5	2,000	0.497177	994	3,265	0.497177	1,623
			365			365

The profitability index identifies which project has the highest ranking. It is calculated as follows:

$$\text{Profitability index (PI)} = \frac{\text{Net present value (NPV)}}{\text{Cost of Investment}} \times 100$$

$$\text{Project 1 PI} = \frac{365}{6,000} \times 100 = 6.08$$

$$\text{Project 2 PI} = \frac{365}{12,000} \times 100 = 3.04$$

We can now see that Project 2 is the clear winner with a PI of 6.08 – exactly twice that of Project 1. While negative PIs are possible, these indicate a project with a negative NPV, which would not be acceptable at the DCF stage.

Summary

We have seen three different methods for evaluating capital projects. My suggestion is that you use Methods 1 and 2 to determine whether a project passes over the average-rate-of-return-and-payback 'hurdles' before subjecting them to the DCF/PI test. If your chosen project survives all these, you can rest assured it will improve your business.

Where can I get further help?

You should look at the following:

■ Read *Financial Management for the Small Business* by Colin Barrow (Kogan Page, 1995).

■ Read *Business Accounting*, 1 and 2, by Frank Wood (Pitman Publishing, 1996).

CHAPTER SIX

Questions on buying a business

FAQ 34

'How do you buy a business?'

What do I need to know?

Logic tells us that buying a business should be the opposite of selling a business. In many ways this is quite correct and much of the process is the same, except that the roles are reversed. The onus is on you, as a buyer, to:

- Find a suitable business to acquire.
- Establish how good it is.
- Decide how much it is worth to you.
- Negotiate with the seller to acquire at the price you want to pay.
- Secure the funding required.
- Integrate the new business within your business to maximise profitability.

Before we start to look at these aspects in detail, I must pass on to you the observations of other business people whom I have known who have bought and sold businesses. The consensus seems to be that the more times you do it the better you get at it. What this does tend to suggest is that if you only ever buy one business you are unlikely to get it completely right – you might pay too much, pick a poor business, or fail to integrate it with your existing enterprise. It seems that over time, as you buy businesses, you refine your approach and tend to get all these aspects right eventually. Also, from my own experience, I know that you have to look at a lot of businesses before you find one that is worth making an offer for.

Finding a suitable business

You will find businesses for sale in a wide range of daily and weekly publications. These range from *Daltons* and *Exchange and Mart*, which are good for retail businesses, to the broadsheets such as the *Telegraph*, *Times* and *Financial Times*, which are good for manufacturing and service businesses. In addition you will find trade-specific publications that also include adverts for businesses for sale. You will also find businesses for sale via the Internet. While I am sure that these all serve some purpose, I am not quite convinced that this is how I would try to find a business that I wanted to buy – it's a bit hit-or-miss and very time consuming for potentially very little reward.

My preferred option would be to choose a trusted or recommended intermediary. This could be your accountant or solicitor or someone they or a trusted business friend might suggest. This way you are dealing with one person who knows what you are looking for, has a reputation to protect, and will put forward to you only businesses that they know to be worthwhile. In effect, a lot of the filtering has been done for you. The end result is, hopefully, one or more businesses that you want to find out more about.

Establishing how good it is

Assuming you know something about the marketplace in which the prospective acquisition operates, you need to find out how good a buy the business may be. You will find that most serious sellers of businesses have already put together a basic seller's pack. This will usually be a one- or two-page overview. It will not state the business name but it will give some basic data, such as turnover, gross margin, pretax profit, number of employees, facilities, business type, geographical location (but probably not town), reason for sale, asking price. If this still interests you and you want to know more you will have to approach the person or organisation shown in the details you have received.

You will usually find that you are dealing with either a firm of accountants or a selling agent. In either case they will want to check out how serious (and knowledgeable) you are before they will send you anything. Ideally, they want to de dealing with principals (the buyer) or their professional advisers. Before they will send you any further information, which is likely to be confidential, they will ask you to sign a confidentiality agreement. This is a legally binding document under which you agree not to disclose any of the confidential information you will receive to any other party without authority. You can understand the seller's position – they don't want to be giving out their secrets to their competitors or any other nosy individuals.

Do bear in mind that what you are going to receive is information that shows the business in its most positive light. There will not be any lies but there may be omissions. If I were buying a business I would want to know the following:

- **Historical financial performance** – certainly at least the last two years' detailed profit and loss statements and balance sheets. In addition I would want to see at least the last five years' figures summarised (e.g., turnover, gross profit, net profit etc.).

- **Current year's budget and performance to date** – this would let me know how well the business is currently performing and what it expects to do for the remainder of the financial year.

- **Statement of resources** – this would let me know what facilities they have (offices and production capacity/equipment) and how good these are (age and specification). It should also include a full break-down of the workforce (e.g., age, skills, what they currently do in the business, length of service with business, salary). I know it may sound heartless but if you are going to buy a business there is a strong possibility that some people may have to be made redundant, so having this information will help you work out how much this will cost you.

- **Products or services** – this should include specification sheets and brochures if they exist. Also, it should provide details of how long these products or services have been offered and what changes have been made over the years (and any proposed) so you can form a view on how good they are.

- **Customer base** – this will be a touchy area so be prepared for a total lack of names of customers. However, they should be able to tell you how much the major customers bought over, say, the last two years and how many customers they have and their average turnover. You will also want to know about any contractual arrangement the business may have with any of its customers.

■ **Order book** – this is a vital health indicator. If the business has no order book then you are buying nothing other than the possibility of selling to previous customers. If the business has a six-month order book then you have at least some firm future.

■ **Contingencies** – you will want to know about anything nasty that may be about to crawl out of the woodwork. Are any suppliers threatening or obtaining judgments against the business for non-payment? Does the bank (or anyone else) have a charge over any of the assets – particularly fixed assets, stock and debtors? Will they release these when you acquire the business. Do any customers have claims against the business for faulty goods? Are there any bad debts? These are just some of the main questions you may want answers to. You will want the seller to warrant these – assure you in writing that what they are saying is the truth.

■ **Competitor/market analysis** – it would be nice to think that this was available for the business that you are thinking of buying – but it probably will not be. So ask the sellers who their competitors are and how big they think their marketplace is.

Armed with this information you can start to form a view of how good the business appears to be. You should be able to eliminate the real no-hopers at this stage. Hopefully, you will see something in the business that makes you feel that you have found a genuine business with some real potential. The next stage is to work out how much it is worth to you.

Deciding how much it is worth to you

Needless to say you must work out what the business you want to buy is worth to you, which is not necessarily the same as what the seller wants (usually lower). However, the factors that will determine the value of the business are the same as those used to sell a business, which is covered in FAQ 20. I would however suggest that you pay particular attention to your evaluation of maintainable profits. As a result of your calculations you will arrive at what the business is worth to you.

Negotiating with the seller and doing the deal

If your valuation of the business and the seller's are the same then a deal will be quickly struck. However, the reality is that you will value the business somewhat lower than the seller. Suppose that you valued the business at £1 million and the seller thinks it is worth £2 million – then the difference in expectations is probably too much for a deal to be done. You might put the offer in writing (subject to plenty of legal get-out clauses) and see what happens. You will probably follow it up with a phone call to discuss it further but it will probably be rejected.

Let's suppose that your valuation of the business is £1.75 million and the seller wants £2 million. Then I would suggest that, since the difference is only 12.5 per cent, a deal can be struck. Do remember that both buyer and seller each have their own highest and lowest price respectively. If the seller needs £2 million pounds to provide for their retirement then that needs to be met somehow. It may be possible to meet this requirement by some clever payment arrangement. If, however, the seller needs £2 million to buy another business then there may not be any scope to come down from this figure without involving another third party. Find out why the buyer has set their selling price and how critical it is to their other plans. If the price is set in stone then you will need to find some area to negotiate on if you still want the business.

However, the selling price may be just one part of the deal that you both need to feel comfortable with. Let us now look at the other considerations for both parties that will need to be dealt with.

Basis and timing of payment

After agreement has been reached on the selling price, then payment could be due in one of several ways. If you have had to pay top value for the business then it should be possible to negotiate stage payments (e.g., 25 per cent on completion with the remaining 75 per cent payable in instalments). This could be based on business performance, e.g., if the business achieves agreed turnover and net profit figures during the next year, then the remaining purchase price would be payable. Alternatively, the remaining price could be paid over an agreed period of time, say in six monthly instalments.

If some form of stage or conditional payment has been agreed, then the seller will want some security to cover this. First, they will have a contract that lays down the agreed basis. However, to give them extra comfort the remaining equity (over and above the initial 25 per cent paid for) could be subject to either a 'right to purchase' or a 'lien or legal charge'. In other words, you as the purchaser have a contractual right and obligation to buy the remaining 75 per cent (right to purchase). Alternatively, you as the buyer acquire all the equity but until you pay for the remaining 75 per cent the seller retains voting control and can seize these shares back until they are paid for.

Which assets are to be included?

Regardless of whether or not the asking price is paid, there is always scope for some of the assets to be excluded from the deal. In fact as buyer you should be very careful to ensure that you are acquiring ownership of everything you think you are entitled to. Do check ownership of every key operational asset to make sure that it will become yours or that the lease can be passed on to you. If a business operates from freehold premises and these are a substantial part of the purchase price you may not want to take this on – either because you want to relocate the business or have a policy of renting assets to maintain flexibility.

It may be possible to agree not to buy or let the seller be your landlord. This is frequently done – the bank will always lend against freehold property with a tenant.

Tie-in of owner-manager

During the first six to twelve months it is absolutely critical that the new business should perform to expectations. Most small businesses are still very dependent on their owner-manager. So during this critical period you may want to keep them on board until you can really get to grips with the business. It is usual practice to tie in the owner-manager in one of two ways. First, give them an employment contract for, say, two years. This keeps them within the business and legally prevents them from setting up in competition to you. You then keep them for however long you need them, which is typically twelve months, and then pay them off for the rest of the contract. Alternatively you can put them on 'gardening leave', whereby you pay them but they stay at home. Once again, this prevents them from setting up in competition to you.

The second, and least favoured option, is to try to construct a no-competition clause in the purchase contract. In other words, you take the view that you have no use for them within the business after you buy it but you do not want them setting up in competition against you straightaway. In effect, you need a head start. My own experience is that these sorts of contract are doomed to failure. Ideally you would want a clause that prevents the seller from setting up in a similar business in your geographic area within, say, twelve months. Such a contract would probably fail at law because it would be deemed to be unfair restraint of trade – you can't prevent a person from carrying out their own trade.

To tie in the owner-manager that you are buying from you really need some leverage. The best leverage is to ensure that some significant element of the purchase price remains unpaid for a period of twelve months. This way it is in their own best interest to ensure that they do what you want them to. It is not uncommon to insert into the purchase contract a bonus (or ratchet) agreement that incentivises them to perform.

Securing the customer base

I don't want to sound too alarming but the customer base is absolutely vital to the future of the business. If it walks with the seller then you have real problems. Ensure that all key accounts are tied into the business. If there are no contracts then either get some in quick or look at some other way of securing the customer base. In most service-type businesses it is not uncommon to have contracts. If, however, you cannot tie in the customers with a watertight contract then isolate them from the seller in some way.

When I ran an advertising agency I had a policy of what I called 'three points of contact' with every client. The purpose of this was to ensure that the client knew they were dealing with a larger professional organisation behind the account handler that they had day-to-day contact with. Every three months each client would be receive a 'courtesy' visit from me to make sure that everything was OK – it also gave me a chance to sell to them. At the same time I made sure the creative director (whom I trusted implicitly) also contacted them on a regular basis. That way we hoped that our clients would feel as if they were part of a bigger family – they knew at least three people within our business. We also made sure that we knew and had contact with more than one person within their business. Of course, the proof of the pudding is in the eating – or testing, in our case. One of our account handlers left and tried to take their key accounts with them. I made some phone calls and visited the clients involved to fly the flag and reinforce how dealing with us would be better than dealing with a freelancer. Fortunately, we kept all the key accounts.

In summary, I would say that you must do your best to secure the customer base. Contracts can work but, if a customer wants to leave, they will, and there is very little you can do to stop them. If there is financial loss as a result of a breach of contract, then you should negotiate a settlement – try to avoid going to court, because nobody really wins.

Securing the key staff

The last thing you need is for the key staff to walk as soon as you buy the business. This could happen for a whole raft of reasons. When it becomes public knowledge that you are going to buy the business you should interview all the key staff to find out what their concerns may be. There will probably be uncertainty and a feeling of loyalty to the departing owner-manager. They will want reassurance that they are not going to lose their jobs. It is possible that they do not have formal contracts of employment, in which case a reassuring move will be to offer them contracts of employment that give both parties security. If key staff are planning to leave then try to identify them early so you can respond quickly to limit the damage.

Securing the funding

I know this may sound stupid but do not leave this vital stage till last. The sensible thing is to talk to your financial backers (assuming you need financial help) before you start to look for a business to buy. The chances are that a variety of longer-term funding may be required so that you may need the support of more than one party. Do look at FAQs 17 to 23 on longer-term funding if you need help. At the minimum you will need a business plan that shows your business and the business you are buying and how they will improve as a result of the acquisition. In fact, regardless of whether or not you need outside funding, you should prepare a business plan for the enlarged business just to make sure it makes the sense you think it does.

You should aim to get yourself into a position where you have negotiated the funding and have a letter of intent. Make sure they are aware of the likely time scales involved so that when you need the money it is available. Do remember that, as well as the purchase price, you will need additional working capital. You will be surprised how many times I have seen people buy a business and then struggle because the increased debtors and stock are way beyond their current banking facilities.

Integrating the new business

Assuming that you have an existing business that you want to integrate with the new business, then you must consider this at the time of negotiation. Some years ago I was tasked with negotiating the deal to acquire a software company on the southeast coast for a business based in Buckinghamshire. My chairman had met up with our stockbrokers and they had agreed that a marriage between the two businesses made sense. There would be no problem in getting the money to buy out the business, subject to my finalising the deal. I met up with their managing director and finance director, who came armed with hundreds of business plans, financial projections and annual accounts. We did talk numbers but my most immediate concern was how the two businesses could be integrated.

I had serious reservations about the roles for some of their board members – for a start we did not need two finance directors! Also, I had concerns about managing a bigger business that was spread out over two sites about a hundred miles apart – we found it difficult enough to manage and control *one* office. My final concern was over the two different cultures within the businesses. We were more formal and structured, whereas they were very laid back with an apparent lack of management. After some deliberation I felt that we would probably fail to integrate the two businesses. We certainly could not relocate their business so there would always be some element of 'us and them'. In the end I had to recommend to the board that we not buy.

I guess the moral of my story is that you cannot just weld two businesses together and expect the resultant hybrid to work. If you want synergy to work, then there needs to be some strong element of compatibility and a thought-out plan as to how this will be brought about. It is hard work!

Where can I get further help?

You should look at the following:

> ■ Contact your accountant, financial adviser, financial backers.
>
> ■ Read *The Best-Laid Business Plans* by Paul Barrow (Virgin Publishing, 2001).
>
> ■ 'How much should I pay to buy a lossmaking business?' (FAQ 35)

FAQ 35

'How much should I pay to buy a lossmaking business?'

What do I need to know?

I know it sounds obvious but you must ask yourself the question, 'Why am I considering buying this business?' There are two possible answers to this question, which are:

1 as a stand-alone investment, which you will leave alone and do nothing with
2 as a means to improve both this and another business which you may already have

If you want to buy it for the first reason then there is no good reason to pay anything for a lossmaking business. If, however, you can improve both the business you are buying and some other business that you may already have then you really should be prepared to pay a premium for it. So what are the good reasons for paying good money for a lossmaking business? Here are just a few good reasons for consolidating two businesses:

> ■ To grow your turnover to achieve a bigger presence in the marketplace – people start to take you seriously.
>
> ■ To improve your buying power with key suppliers – suppliers start actively to want your business and offer discounts.
>
> ■ To make cost savings and improve the profitability of both businesses – shared administration costs, shared management, shared premises etc.
>
> ■ To share expertise to grow both businesses faster.
>
> ■ To remove a competitor who may be driving down prices and hence reducing your profitability.
>
> ■ To make your business bigger and more profitable ready for sale to a trade buyer.

There are, as you can see, many good reasons for acquiring a loss-making business – and I am sure you can probably think of some more.

How much should I pay?

The answer is a question: how much is it worth to you? You must look at what you can do with the business you are buying to see how you can either make it profitable or use it to improve the combined businesses that you now have.

An example with some numbers

You have the opportunity to buy a printing business which last year on a turnover of £1 million made a net loss of £40,000. The owner wants £1 million to acquire the business, which has no significant net assets on the balance sheet. You have the following information about the business:

Last year's profit and loss statement – for the business being acquired		
Sales		1,000,000
Cost of sales (materials)	60%	600,000
Gross margin		400,000
Overheads:		
Administration		75,000
Management		150,000
Directors		150,000
Rent, rates etc.		50,000
Depreciation		15,000
		440,000
Net profit		−40,000

You have found out that if you acquired the business, which offers an identical product to yours and shares many of your customers, immediate cost savings could be made. Below is a summary of the changes that could be made within three months and the benefits the new combined business would receive:

a. Combined purchasing of materials would reduce cost from 60 per cent of sales to 55 per cent for both businesses.
b. By combining sales of both products, selling prices could be increased by 5 per cent, because of the reduction in competition.

c. Administration staff costs could be reduced by £25,000 per annum (one person) with a redundancy cost of £3,000.

d. Management staff costs could be reduced by £75,000 per annum (two persons) with a redundancy cost of £10,000.

e. The co-director of the acquired business (the owner-manager's partner) would not need to be employed in the new business. This would save £75,000 per annum but cost £25,000 in redundancy costs.

f. There is room for both businesses to trade from the same premises. Preliminary discussions with the landlord have indicated that he would release the business being acquired from its lease for a payment of £100,000. Relocating the businesses on one site would not increase any other rent and rates figures.

In addition, your own business for the same period has the following trading information.

Last year's profit and loss statement – for the acquiring business		
Sales		4,000,000
Cost of sales	60%	2,400,000
Gross margin		1,600,000
Overheads:		
Administration		150,000
Management		300,000
Directors		200,000
Rent, Rates etc.		150,000
Depreciation		45,000
		845,000
Net profit		755,000

The next stage is to ascertain how a combination of the two businesses would perform assuming that all the profit improvement changes – a. to f. above – have been put in place. Assuming everything went to plan, then after three months the following is how the combined business could look.

Bolting two businesses together

		New		Existing		Combined
Sales		1,000,000		4,000,000		5,000,000
Cost of sales	60%	600,000	60%	2,400,000	55%	2,750,000
Gross margin		400,000		1,600,000		2,250,000
Price increase					5%	250,000
Improved gross margin						2,500,000
Overheads:						
Administration		75,000		150,000		200,000
Management		150,000		300,000		375,000
Directors		150,000		200,000		275,000
Rent, rates etc.		50,000		150,000		150,000
Depreciation		15,000		45,000		60,000
		440,000		845,000		1,060,000
Net profit		−40,000		755,000		1,190,000
P/E multiple		n/a		6		6
Value of business		n/a		4,530,000		7,140,000

As a result of combining the two businesses, a new business with a turnover of £5 million with reduced costs is now capable of producing net profit of £1,190,000 in a full year. This is an improvement of £435,000 per annum (£1,190,000 − £755,000) achieved by combining the two businesses. You will see that, using a P/E multiple of six, the value of the new combined business is £7,140,000, which is an improvement of £2,610,000 (£435,000 × 6).

So, on the face of things, by combining the two businesses a new enterprise is created that is worth some £2,160,000 more than before. In principle it is worth paying up to this amount to acquire the business, less the costs involved in achieving this. The table below shows these and the maximum price that can be justified for buying the business.

Value versus cost of acquisition

Improved business worth		2,610,000
Costs:		
Admin redundancies	3,000	
Management redundancies	10,000	
Directors' redundancies	25,000	
Compensation to landlord	100,000	
	138,000	
Maximum justifiable price to pay		2,472,000

Assuming costs of some £138,000, which should be deducted from the value of the deal, then the maximum justifiable purchase price is around £2,472,000.

So, based on this calculation, how does a purchase price of £1 million, as wanted by the seller, sound? I think the conclusion must be that it looks to be pretty good value because of the improvement it helps make to the combined business. The message must therefore be that lossmaking businesses are worth buying for an apparent premium if you can improve them and any other associated businesses.

Tax losses

Another sound reason for buying a business is the availability of tax losses. For example, the business in the example we have just seen has lost £40,000 in the last year alone. It may have several years of losses that have some value to an acquiring business that is profitable. If you buy a business that is in a similar trade to your own then its tax losses can be offset against your future profits. This is worth paying for, as long as you pay less than your future tax rate. If, say, your business pays tax at an average rate of 30 per cent and a business you are buying has tax losses of £100,000 then this is worth up to £30,000 (£100,000 @ 30 per cent) to your business. This may be another 'sweetener' for buying a lossmaking business.

Where can I get further help?

You should look at the following:

- Contact your accountant, financial adviser, financial backers.
- Read *The Best-Laid Business Plans* by Paul Barrow (Virgin Publishing, 2001).
- 'How do you buy a business?' (FAQ 34)

FAQ 36

'How do I make sure that there are no nasty surprises after I have bought a business?'

What do I need to know?

When you buy a business most of the work that you will have done will be based on making sure that you have agreed to pay the right price for

the business as you see it. If you have followed most of what was outlined in FAQ 34, 'How do you buy a business?', then you should not
go too far wrong. However, when you are relying on the word of other
people, especially those who are trying to sell you the business, then you
have a right to be both suspicious and cautious. You should not take at
face value any information you are given by the seller. To further
improve your chances and reduce the possibility even further of your
being sold a pup, there are some additional things that you should do:

- Obtain a warranty from the seller that all critical facts are correct.
- Obtain a third-party verification of all assets and liabilities (balance sheet audit).
- Obtain a third-party verification of any financial forecasts.
- Obtain the best tax and legal advice you can afford.
- Run your proposed acquisition by as many people as possible to get their feedback.

If you have done this and your proposed acquisition gets the
thumbs-up, then you can be as sure as possible that you have done all
the right things. Let's have a look at each of these in just a little detail
so that you know what to look out for.

Warranties

A warranty can be defined as a statement made in a contract that, if
unfulfilled, does not usually invalidate the contract but could lead to
the payment of damages. If the warranty is clearly stated in writing it
is known as an **express warranty** and if it is not but is understood by
both parties it is known as an **implied warranty**.

So how do you as the buyer make use of this? The answer is to
make sure that you question every statement of fact and ignore every
statement of opinion. So, if the seller makes any statement that is
important, and may influence your decision to buy, ask them to provide the proof to back up it up, and if there is still any uncertainty ask
them to provide a warranty in the sale contract. The warranty should
be given by the directors of the company (in the case of a limited
company) or by the proprietor or partners (in the case of an unincor-
porated business).

Let's have a look at how this might work in practice. You are buying a business but have a concern about the level of returned goods and

other outstanding claims that customers may have against the business. Your big concern is that a major customer may have a valid but as yet undisclosed or unknown action against the business. Potentially, this could lead to non-payment of a large sum of money and a claim for damages for consequential loss. If this situation were to materialise the business would be worth considerably less than the current price.

Under these circumstances, you need a warranty in writing within the sale contract. In essence, this will state that the directors warrant that there are no outstanding actions either already commenced or about to be commenced for faulty or non-delivered goods and any consequential liability caused by this. The warranty would be valid for, say, two years. Should any of the stated events occur then you have the comfort of knowing that you will be able to claim damages for the effect of this on the business.

As a final option, you may want a small part of the purchase price to be held back from the sellers until the warranty period has expired. Normally, this would not be an acceptable course of action, but if there are some very real concerns (based on previous experience) then holding back, say, 10 per cent of the purchase price will give you some extra comfort.

Balance sheet audit
While the seller will provide historic financial information in the form of audited accounts and management accounts, there will be a gap between audited figures and the current position. The concern must be that in the period, say six months, since the last audited balance sheet things have changed. For example, assets may have been sold; levels of debtors may not be as high (or as sound) as stated; levels of creditors may be higher than stated. You need confirmation of the state of play today. The way that you achieve this is to employ an independent accountant (your auditor will do it) to carry out a balance sheet audit.

The balance sheet audit will systematically construct and verify the balance sheet for the business you are buying. This will be done from the records that the business has. In addition your accountant will seek third-party verification of the figures. For example, let us say the business has debtors of £200,000. By any account, this is a very significant asset and you would want to make sure that this value was correct and it was all fairly current and collectable. Your accountant will take the debtor list if there is one, or create it if there is not one. Then the accountant will write to a selection of these debtors (debtor circulation) to ask them to confirm how much they owe the business and the age of this debt. The business will send out the debtor circulation letter (on their headed notepaper), but authorising the debtor to return the information required directly to your accountant.

A similar approach will be taken to other critical figures within the balance sheet – bank balance, hire purchase, trade creditors etc. As a result of the balance sheet audit you should then feel very confident in the figures you now have. Of course, if the negotiations go on for some time the value of this activity may diminish because some months may pass by. You should leave this activity as late as possible. If there is a gap between the balance sheet audit date and the final date of completion, ask the directors to warrant the changes.

Verify the financial forecasts

It is quite possible that the sellers of the business you are interested in have prepared budget figures, which they have shown you. Obviously, they are holding out to you that this is their view of how the business is going to perform over the next twelve months. There is a strong chance that you may be influenced by these figures, especially if they are designed to make you believe that the business is going to grow sales and profits substantially. I guess I would equate this to a used-car salesman saying to you (about the car you are interested in), 'It's a lovely little runner, three careful owners, only done forty-five thousand miles and does fifty miles to the gallon.' I think I would want to see some proof of this and I might want a mechanic to check out the condition of the car.

So how do you check out any profit and cash flow forecasts that you are shown? Once again I would enlist the support of an independent accountant (your accountant). They have the skills to verify the forecasts – in fact they could do it at the same time as they are doing the balance sheet audit. In essence they will audit the forecasts to check that:

- The calculations are correct – it's quite amazing how many errors there are in spreadsheet projections.

- The basis on which assumption have been made are correct – e.g., if the cash flow shows that debtors are paid in 30 days a check is made to verify that in the past debtors have paid in 30 days. If historically they have paid in 60 days then the cash flow is going to be too optimistic.

■ The sales growth is realistic – no one can guarantee sales growth but it is possible to state whether the projected sales growth has any semblance of reality. This will be done by looking at historic growth – e.g., if in the past average sales growth has been 10 per cent per annum and the sales projections show 30 per cent for this year, then my immediate thought would be 'no way'.

The objective of verifying the financial projections is to increase the level of confidence in the financial prospects of the business.

Take tax and legal advice

I suspect that your knowledge of tax and law is somewhere between 'not a lot' and 'even less than not a lot'. I am a chartered accountant with a reasonable working knowledge of most business-related accounting, finance, tax and law, but I would always take advice if I were spending large amounts of money. There are pitfalls at every corner when buying a business. I think you will agree that the contract itself, together with any warranties, does need the skills of a good commercial solicitor. It is a specialist job – so don't see the solicitor who did your conveyancing on your house. You will pay considerably more for a commercial solicitor, but they have done what you require hundreds of times before – so they know all the wheezes. If you use a good solicitor then you should not go too far wrong.

You may wonder why you need tax advice if you are buying a business. You certainly need it if you are selling a business – to make sure that you end up with more of the sales proceeds than the tax man does. However, even buying a business can be a tax minefield, especially if you are buying it from a sole trader or partnership. The main issues are:

■ **Past tax history of the business**. Have all the taxes been paid and are there any outstanding Inland Revenue enquiries? Is anything going to crawl out of the woodwork and bite you? With a limited company, payment of tax is relatively straightforward: the company pays it. With sole traders and partnerships, it is significantly more complicated because the business does not pay the tax – the individuals do and there may be little proof of this.

■ **Current year's tax computation**. Has this been correctly calculated and agreed with the Inland Revenue?

Tax losses. If you are buying a business with tax losses, are these transferable to your business?

In addition, there may be PAYE issues that need clarifying. For instance, a friend of mine ran a business in which they used about fifty self-employed salespeople. They did this because it made it easier to get rid of them and also it saved on NI contributions and was easier to administer. They also did not deduct tax from their payments. The Inland Revenue had constantly challenged this arrangement on the basis that these salespeople were really employees and as such should be liable for PAYE and NI. There was also the threat that, had any of these salespeople not paid their tax, the company would be liable for its payment. Someday, the feeling was, the Inland Revenue would have its way and a large tax bill would land on the company's doorstep.

Using professionals in an area that you have little knowledge of is only common sense. The cost will be far outweighed by the benefit.

Get others whom you trust to check out your plan
I am really suggesting that you get a second, third and fourth opinion from as many people as you can. The reasoning behind this is that if more than one person views the proposition any glaring faults in your reasoning will be spotted. Don't get them to look at the technical stuff (contract, audited accounts) – unless they ask and have knowledge of these areas. Ask them for their opinion/comments on the overall idea of buying this business (or even any business). You may be surprised at the very practical comments that they will make.

If you're a man and married, ask your wife what she thinks of the idea. I am a great believer in women's intuition. They are great at judging people. My ex-wife was extremely perceptive and would comment to me, on meeting someone for the first time, 'I don't trust him – be careful.' On every occasion she was correct. The problem is that you are always too close to the situation and want it to be right.

Talk with any business colleagues you may have to see if they have bought a business before, and ask them what pitfalls they encountered. My own experience is that buying a business is a risky and difficult process and if you can get input from as many people as possible you will minimise the chances of failure. My own view is that you improve with experience at buying businesses.

Where can I get further help?

You should look at the following:

- Contact your accountant, financial adviser, financial backers.
- Read *The Best-Laid Business Plans* by Paul Barrow (Virgin Publishing, 2001).
- 'How do you buy a business?' (FAQ 34)

FAQ 37

'Which is easier/better: organic growth or growth through acquisition?'

What do I need to know?

I suppose that any business looking for accelerated growth is entitled to consider all the options. If that business is profitable and cash-rich (or has access to funding) then there are two recognised methods of achieving this:

1. Growing your own business – otherwise known as **organic growth**. This is where an enterprise concentrates all its resources on growing its own core business. This can be achieved by doing more of the same or diversification.
2. Growing through **acquisition**. This in effect is recognising that organic growth is not possible or will not happen quickly enough. This can involve acquiring a similar business (doing what yours does); a complementary business (fits in below or above yours – vertical integration); or a different type of business (diversification).

The temptation, for those people who believe that organic growth is not happening fast enough or will not enable the business to meet its profit objectives, is to acquire another. Let's have a look at the two options to see their comparative virtues.

Organic growth

Risk

- **Business risk:** without doubt the low-risk option. If you attempt growth through selling more of the same product to similar customers then there is virtually no business risk at all. If, however, you attempt to grow through diversification (i.e. selling totally new products to totally different customers) I would suggest that this is a high-risk activity. This is in effect a new business, using some existing resources but bringing in other new resources.

■ **Funding risk**: if the growth is within the same marketplace (customers and products) then the funding risk is low – you are just buying a bit more of what you are already buying. Your only concern would be cash flow. If the growth is through diversification (new customers and new products) then this is a medium to high funding risk – you will be hiring new people, developing and making unfamiliar products. This will involve the large-scale purchase of assets.

Cost

Organic growth is usually less costly than acquisition. Scaling up in a business can cost only a few thousand pounds. Much of the cost is marginal – a bit more of this and a bit more of that. If the growth is through diversification, then the costs can be more substantial but still only in tens of thousands of pounds.

Return

Scaling up offers very high returns because of the low cost and high returns. Diversification can be quite disappointing and offer lower returns than the core business.

Speed

Most organic growth is relatively slow to yield substantial growth, especially if the business is mature. In newer, more dynamic businesses, where core sales growth is faster, the organic growth is faster but still not capable of doubling turnover in, say, three years. Diversification can be painfully slow.

Ease

Most organic growth is reasonably easy to achieve, especially if you are using the same people and resources. Diversification is more difficult, especially since there is typically a management under-estimation of the task.

Growth through acquisition

Risk

- **Business risk**: potentially very high risk of diversification or vertical integration. The limited knowledge of customers, products, workforce, management, finances etc. of the business being acquired compound this business risk. However, the acquisition of a similar business to your existing enterprise is a medium-business-risk activity – if done in a professional manner. It could be argued that this option is no more risky than organic diversification.

- **Funding risk**: if the growth is through diversification or vertical integration then the funding risk is very high – but it can be reduced depending on how much of the purchase price is for goodwill (to buy the business – high risk) and how much to buy assets (low risk). If the business being acquired is a clone of your existing enterprise, then this is a medium funding risk.

Cost

Undoubtedly the costly option. First, there are the professional fees, which will cost several thousands of pounds. Then there is the cost of the business, which is based on a multiple of profits plus the cost of any assets acquired. Overall it may cost two to three times more to acquire a business than to achieve the same growth organically.

Return

Has the potential to yield very high returns (see FAQ 25) if you buy at the right price and integrate the two businesses successfully.

Speed

Acquisition offers a quick-growth option, which cannot be matched by organic growth. Particularly useful if there is a 'window of opportunity' that must be seized – in most cases organic growth will miss the boat. Can provide a business with a way of doubling sales almost overnight.

Ease

Extremely difficult to integrate a newly acquired business, owing to cultural differences, location, potential management indifference/work overload, stress on systems.

Overall conclusion

It all depends on your business objectives. If you have a business that is profitable with good cash flow and growing at above 20 per cent per annum, then stick with organic growth – you should not be considering acquisition. If your business has slowed down, but is cash-rich (or has access to funds), then acquisition can revitalise it – especially if it buys in better management with the business it is acquiring. The final consideration must be time scale. If your market is changing and your size of business is under threat, then acquisition may be the only way to survive – organic growth will not provide survival.

Where can I get further help?

You should look at the following:

- Contact your accountant, financial adviser, financial backers.
- Read *The Best-Laid Business Plans* by Paul Barrow (Virgin Publishing, 2001).
- Speak to someone who has bought a business.

FAQ 38

'How should I fund a business that I am buying?'

What do I need to know?

Quite frequently when you are looking at buying a business the immediate thought is: I need a lot of money for a risky proposition. The tendency is to focus on the large amount needed and treat the acquisition of the business as one transaction. You will also have read that banks start to feel uncomfortable funding above about £150,000 and the venture capitalists don't really look at propositions below £250,000. This seems to leave a gap right in the area where many small business acquisitions need funding.

So what's the answer if you are trying to fund the acquisition of business? Don't forget that when you buy a business you are taking on all the assets and liabilities. Break down the funding need into smaller sums for different purposes. Work out what assets are being acquired (goodwill, motor vehicles, plant and machinery, debtors, stock etc.) and what liabilities are being taken over (long-term loans, bank overdraft, trade creditors etc.). Then look at appropriate funding for these.

An example with some numbers

You are buying a small engineering business and have reached agreement to pay £280,000. At this level of funding it appears to be beyond traditional bank funding and business-angel funding. It also appears to be right on the margin of venture-capitalist funding. What options are there for funding this acquisition? The balance sheet for the business is as shown below.

Balance sheet @ 31/12/2000		
Fixed assets		
Land and buildings		110,000
Plant and machinery		70,000
Motor vehicles		20,000
		200,000
Current assets		
Debtors	20,000	
Stock and WIP	10,000	
	30,000	
Current Liabilities		
Trade creditors	10,000	
Bank overdraft	20,000	
	30,000	
Net current assets		0
Long-term loan		20,000
Net assets		180,000
Financed by:		
Share capital		80,000
Reserves		100,000
Shareholders' funds		180,000

Remembering what I said earlier, break down the funding need into smaller amounts. On this basis the £280,000 purchase price can be broken down as follows:

Net assets purchase	£180,000
Goodwill	£100,000
Total purchase price	£280,000

Now it becomes clearer (I hope) that there are two distinct funding requirements – £100,000 risk funding (for the goodwill) and £180,000 asset-based funding (for the net assets). Suddenly the funding proposition becomes so much easier because it has been broken down into different amounts for different purposes:

1. Existing funding
The business already has some existing funding, which can continue to be used.

- Bank overdraft and trade creditors – looking at the balance sheet, we can see that there are trade creditors of £10,000 and bank overdraft of £20,000. These are covered by debtors of £20,000 and stock and WIP of £10,000. This can continue.
- Long-term loan – there is a loan of £20,000, which in this case is hire purchase on the motor vehicles. This can continue.

2. New funding
The new funding requirement could be broken down as follows:

- **Goodwill (£100,000)** – this is the only truly risky element of the whole proposition. The bank will not want to fund this unless the acquiring business can offer security to cover it. If the business proposition is good, and you can prove it to the bank but you do not have security, then try a bank loan under the Small Firms Loan Guarantee scheme (see FAQ 23). You should seek to use your own spare cash first. Do not use your own business's cash, or else you will deprive it of working capital. Any element of this that cannot be funded by the bank would be ideal for a business angel to fund.
- **Land and buildings (£110,000)** – since the buildings are fully paid for (there is no mortgage), there are a range of options. The acquiring business could arrange a commercial mortgage on them – although it is unlikely that a lender will offer 100 per cent. However, you, as the owner of the acquiring business, could take this on as a pension-fund asset and rent it back to the business. This will be favourably looked on by most lenders and you may be able to get a 100 per cent mortgage. Another option may be to sell the land and buildings to a third party who will rent them back to you.
- **Plant and machinery (£80,000)** – can be funded in any one of several ways. Hire purchase, bank loan, lease etc. If there are several assets making up this amount they can be split among all these options to spread the risk.

Overall conclusion

What at first seemed like a high-risk £280,000 funding requirement can be split into £100,000 high-risk (for the goodwill), £110,000 very low-risk (for the land and buildings) and £80,000 low-risk (for the plant and machinery). This now becomes a much easier funding proposition once it has been broken down and the risk spread. You need to employ this approach when you are seeking funding for any business you want to acquire.

Where can I get further help?

You should look at the following:

- Contact your accountant, financial adviser, financial backers.
- Read *The Best-Laid Business Plans* by Paul Barrow (Virgin Publishing, 2001).
- Speak to your bank.

Appendix |

FAQ 1

1. Reduced growth

Profit statement

	Month 7	Month 8	Month 9	Month 10	Month 11	Month 12
Sales	11,000	12,000	13,000	14,000	15,000	16,000
Cost of sales:						
Materials	5,500	6,000	6,500	7,000	7,500	8,000
Wages	3,300	3,600	3,900	4,200	4,500	4,800
	8,800	9,600	10,400	11,200	12,000	12,800
Gross profit	2,200	2,400	2,600	2,800	3,000	3,200
Overheads:						
Salaries	750	750	750	750	750	750
Rent, rates etc.	250	250	250	250	250	250
Advertising	150	150	150	150	150	150
Repairs and maintenance	100	100	100	100	100	100
	1,250	1,250	1,250	1,250	1,250	1,250
Net profit	950	1,150	1,350	1,550	1,750	1,950
Net profit – year to date	950	2,100	3,450	5,000	6,750	8,700

Cash flow statement

Receipts:	Month 7	Month 8	Month 9	Month 10	Month 11	Month 12
Cash from debtors (60 days' credit)	10,000	10,000	11,000	12,000	13,000	14,000
Payments:						
Materials (30 days' credit)	5,000	5,500	6,000	6,500	7,000	7,500
Wages (paid in current month)	3,300	3,600	3,900	4,200	4,500	4,800

Cash flow statement – *continued*

Payments – *continued*	Month 7	Month 8	Month 9	Month 10	Month 11	Month 12
Salaries (paid in current month)	750	750	750	750	750	750
Rent, rates etc. (paid in current month)	250	250	250	250	250	250
Advertising (paid in current month)	150	150	150	150	150	150
Repairs and maintenance (30 days' credit)	**100**	100	100	100	100	100
Total cash payments	9,550	10,350	11,150	11,950	12,750	13,550
Net cash flow for month	450	−350	−150	50	250	450
Bank balance	450	100	−50	0	250	700

2. Improved profit

Profit statement

	Month 7	Month 8	Month 9	Month 10	Month 11	Month 12
Sales	13,000	16,000	19,000	22,000	25,000	28,000
Cost of sales:						
Materials	5,850	7,200	8,550	9,900	11,250	12,600
Wages	3,250	4,000	4,750	5,500	6,250	7,000
	9,100	11,200	13,300	15,400	17,500	19,600
Gross profit	3,900	4,800	5,700	6,600	7,500	8,400
Overheads:						
Salaries	750	750	750	750	750	750
Rent, rates etc.	250	250	250	250	250	250
Advertising	150	150	150	150	150	150
Repairs and maintenance	100	100	100	100	100	100
	1,250	1,250	1,250	1,250	1,250	1,250
Net profit	2,650	3,550	4,450	5,350	6,250	7,150
Cumulative net profits	2,650	6,200	10,650	16,000	22,250	29,400

Cash flow statement

Receipts:	Month 7	Month 8	Month 9	Month 10	Month 11	Month 12
Cash from debtors (60 days' credit)	**10,000**	**10,000**	13,000	16,000	19,000	22,000
Payments:						
Materials (30 days' credit)	**5,000**	5,850	7,200	8,550	9,900	11,250
Wages (paid in current month)	3,250	4,000	4,750	5,500	6,250	7,000
Salaries (paid in current month)	750	750	750	750	750	750
Rent, rates etc. (paid in current month)	250	250	250	250	250	250
Advertising (paid in current month)	150	150	150	150	150	150

Cash flow statement – *continued*

	Month 7	Month 8	Month 9	Month 10	Month 11	Month 12
Repairs and maintenance (30 days' credit)	**100**	100	100	100	100	100
Total cash payments	9,500	11,100	13,200	15,300	17,400	19,500
Net cash flow for month	500	–1,100	–200	700	1,600	2,500
Cumulative cash flows	500	–600	–800	–100	1,500	4,000

3. Improved cash flow

Profit statement

	Month 7	Month 8	Month 9	Month 10	Month 11	Month 12
Sales	13,000	16,000	19,000	22,000	25,000	28,000
Cost of sales:						
Materials	6,500	8,000	9,500	11,000	12,500	14,000
Wages	3,900	4,800	5,700	6,600	7,500	8,400
	10,400	12,800	15,200	17,600	20,000	22,400
Gross profit	2,600	3,200	3,800	4,400	5,000	5,600
Overheads:						
Salaries	750	750	750	750	750	750
Rent, rates etc.	250	250	250	250	250	250
Advertising	150	150	150	150	150	150
Repairs and maintenance	100	100	100	100	100	100
	1,250	1,250	1,250	1,250	1,250	1,250
Net profit	1,350	1,950	2,550	3,150	3,750	4,350
Net profit – year to date	1,350	3,300	5,850	9,000	12,750	17,100

Cash flow statement

	Month 7	Month 8	Month 9	Month 10	Month 11	Month 12
Receipts:						
Cash from debtors (30 days' credit)	**10,000**	13,000	16,000	19,000	22,000	25,000
Payments:						
Materials (30 days' credit)	**5,000**	6,500	8,000	9,500	11,000	12,500
Wages (paid in current month)	3,900	4,800	5,700	6,600	7,500	8,400
Salaries (paid in current month)	750	750	750	750	750	750
Rent, rates etc. (paid in current month)	250	250	250	250	250	250
Advertising (paid in current month)	150	150	150	150	150	150
Repairs and maintenance (30 days' credit)	**100**	100	100	100	100	100
Total cash payments	10,150	12,550	14,950	17,350	19,750	22,150
Net cash flow for month	–150	450	1,050	1,650	2,250	2,850
Bank balance	–150	300	1,350	3,000	5,250	8,100

FAQ 5

Scenario 2

(First 6 months):
Annualised sales · 168,000 204,000 240,000 250,000 250,000 250,000
Profit forecast

	Month 1	Month 2	Month 3	Month 4	Month 5	Month 6
Sales	14,000	17,000	20,000	20,833	20,833	20,833
Cost of sales:						
Materials	7,000	8,500	10,000	10,417	10,417	10,417
Wages	4,200	5,100	6,000	6,250	6,250	6,250
	11,200	13,600	16,000	16,667	16,667	16,667
Gross profit	2,800	3,400	4,000	4,167	4,167	4,167
Overheads:						
Salaries	750	750	750	750	750	750
Rent, rates etc.	250	250	250	250	250	250
Advertising	150	150	150	150	150	150
Repairs and maintenance	100	100	100	100	100	100
	1,250	1,250	1,250	1,250	1,250	1,250
Net profit	1,550	2,150	2,750	2,917	2,917	2,917

	Previous year						
Cash flow forecast							
Debtors	25,000	28,000	34,000	40,000	41,667	41,667	41,667
Stock and WIP	12,500	14,000	17,000	20,000	20,833	20,833	20,833
Trade creditors	−6,150	−7,100	−8,600	−10,100	−10,517	−10,517	−10,517
Bank overdraft	−16,350	−16,350	−16,350	−16,350	−16,350	−16,350	−16,350
Net working capital required	15,000	18,550	26,050	33,550	35,633	35,633	35,633
+/(−) Net working capital	0	3,550	7,500	7,500	2,083	0	0
Capital expenditure	0	25,000	0	0	0	0	0
Less: net profit	−15,000	−1,550	−2,150	−2,750	−2,917	−2,917	−2,917
Net cash (in)/out	0	27,000	5,350	4,750	−833	−2,917	−2,917
Additional funding required		27,000	32,350	37,100	36,267	33,350	30,433

(Second 6 months):

| Annualised sales | 250,000 | 250,000 | 250,000 | 250,000 | 250,000 | 250,000 | |

Profit forecast

	Month 7	Month 8	Month 9	Month 10	Month 11	Month 12	Total
Sales	20,833	20,833	20,833	20,833	20,833	20,833	238,500
Cost of sales:							
Materials	10,417	10,417	10,417	10,417	10,417	10,417	119,250
Wages	6,250	6,250	6,250	6,250	6,250	6,250	71,550
	16,667	16,667	16,667	16,667	16,667	16,667	90,800
Gross profit	4,167	4,167	4,167	4,167	4,167	4,167	47,700
Overheads:							
Salaries	750	750	750	750	750	750	9,000
Rent, rates etc.	250	250	250	250	250	250	3,000
Advertising	150	150	150	150	150	150	1,800
Repairs and							
maintenance	100	100	100	100	100	100	1,200
	1,250	1,250	1,250	1,250	1,250	1,250	15,000
Net profit	2,917	2,917	2,917	2,917	2,917	2,917	32,700

Cash flow forecast

Debtors	41,667	41,667	41,667	41,667	41,667	41,667	
Stock and WIP	20,833	20,833	20,833	20,833	20,833	20,833	
Trade creditors	−10,517	−10,517	−10,517	−10,517	−10,517	−10,517	
Bank overdraft	−16,350	−16,350	−16,350	−16,350	−16,350	−16,350	
Net working capital							
required	35,633	35,633	35,633	35,633	35,633	35,633	
+/(−) Net working							
capital	0	0	0	0	0	0	
Capital expenditure	0	0	0	0	0	0	
Less: net profit	−2,917	−2,917	−2,917	−2,917	−2,917	−2,917	
Net cash (in)/out	−2,917	−2,917	−2,917	−2,917	−2,917	−2,917	
Additional funding							
required	27,517	24,600	21,683	18,767	15,850	12,933	26,487

FAQ 14

'Quick' profit report

	Month 1	Month 2	Month 3	Month 4	Month 5	Month 6	Month 7	Month 8	Month 9	Month 10	Month 11	Month 12
(1) Sales £												
(2) Gross margin %												
(3) Fixed costs £												
(4) Break-even point = (3) divided by (2) £												
(5) Break-even gap = (1) less (5) £												
(6) Quick profit/loss = (5) times (2) £												
(7) Margin of safety = (5) divided by (1) times 100 %												

FAQ 24

Modern-style presentation of Precision Engineering Ltd balance sheet

Precision Engineering Ltd – balance sheet @ 31/12/200

Fixed assets (or tangible assets)		
Land and buildings (1%)		30,000
Plant and machinery (20%)		10,000
Fixtures and fittings (25%)		3,000
		43,000
Intangible assets		
Goodwill		20,000
R&D		10,000
Patents, trade marks etc.		5,000
		35,000
Current assets		
Stock and WIP	5,000	
Debtors	10,000	
Prepayments	200	
Bank balance	0	
	15,200	
Current liabilities < 12 months		
PAYE/NI etc.	1,000	
Trade creditors	5,000	
Accruals	500	
Bank overdraft	5,000	
	11,500	
Net current assets		**3,700**
Long-term loans > 12 months		
Hire purchase		1,000
Director's loan		10,000
Mortgage		15,000
		26,000
Net assets		**55,700**
Shareholders' funds		
Share capital		10,000
Reserves		45,700
		55,700

FAQs 33 to 38

Ratios example using the accounts for Mark Engineering Ltd

Mark Engineering Ltd

Profit and loss account for year to 31 March 2001

		2001		2000
Sales:		185,000		160,000
Cost of sales:				
Opening stock	7,000		6,000	
Materials purchased	30,000		25,000	
	37,000		31,000	
Less: closing stock	−10,000		−7,000	
Material costs	27,000		24,000	
Heat & light	8,865		8,500	
Wages (incl. NI)	44,080		42,000	
Cost of sales		79,945		74,500
Gross profit		105,055		85,500
Expenses:				
Directors' salaries (incl. NI)	38,570		38,000	
Clerk's wages	2,500		2,500	
Rent and rates	18,000		17,500	
Heat and light	1,500		1,400	
Postage and stationery	1,000		1,000	
Sundry expense	500		400	
Bank charges	600		800	
Motor expenses	7,000		6,500	
Depreciation	10,000		10,000	
		79,670		78,100
Operating profit (or trading profit)		25,385		7,400
Bank and loan interest		500		2,000
Net profit before tax (PBT)		24,885		5,400
Tax provision		6,220		1,350
Net profit/(loss) after tax (PAT)		18,665		4,050

Note: In 2001 there were five full-time employees in the company (in 2000 there were four full-time employees).

Mark Engineering Ltd

Balance sheet as at
31 March 2001

			2001		2000
Fixed assets:					
Plant and equipment			12,500		22,500
Current assets:					
Stock	10,000			7,000	
Debtors	13,000			10,000	
Cash	100	23,100		50	17,050
Less: creditors (due less than 12 months):					
(or current liabilities)					
Overdraft	5,000			13,050	
Creditors	1,690	6,690		2,000	15,050
Net current assets:			16,410		2,000
Total assets less current liabilities: (or capital employed)			28,910		24,500
Less: creditors (due more than 12 months)			10,000		24,255
Net assets			18,910		245
Capital and reserves					
Share capital			10,000		10,000
Reserves (include. P&L account)			8,910		−9,755
Shareholders' funds (or net worth)			18,910		245

FAQ 38

Present-value tables for use with discounted cash flow calculations

Year	1%	2%	3%	4%	5%	6%	7%	8%	9%	10%
1	0.990099	0.980392	0.970874	0.961538	0.952381	0.943396	0.934579	0.925926	0.917431	0.909091
2	0.980296	0.961169	0.942596	0.924556	0.907029	0.889996	0.873439	0.857339	0.841680	0.826446
3	0.970590	0.942322	0.915142	0.888996	0.863838	0.839619	0.816298	0.793832	0.772183	0.751315
4	0.960980	0.923845	0.888487	0.854804	0.822702	0.792094	0.762895	0.735030	0.708425	0.683013
5	0.951466	0.905731	0.862609	0.821927	0.783526	0.747258	0.712986	0.680583	0.649931	0.620921
6	0.942045	0.887971	0.837484	0.790315	0.746215	0.704961	0.666342	0.630170	0.596267	0.564474
7	0.932718	0.870560	0.813092	0.759918	0.710681	0.665057	0.622750	0.583490	0.547034	0.513158
8	0.923483	0.853490	0.789409	0.730690	0.676839	0.627412	0.582009	0.540269	0.501866	0.466507
9	0.914340	0.836755	0.766417	0.702587	0.644609	0.591898	0.543934	0.500249	0.460428	0.424098
10	0.905287	0.820348	0.744094	0.675564	0.613913	0.558395	0.508349	0.463193	0.422411	0.385543

Year	11%	12%	13%	14%	15%	16%	17%	18%	19%	20%
1	0.900901	0.892857	0.884956	0.877193	0.869565	0.862069	0.854701	0.847458	0.840336	0.833333
2	0.811622	0.797194	0.783147	0.769468	0.756144	0.743163	0.730514	0.718184	0.706165	0.694444
3	0.731191	0.711780	0.693050	0.674972	0.657516	0.640658	0.624371	0.608631	0.593416	0.578704
4	0.658731	0.635518	0.613319	0.592080	0.571753	0.552291	0.533650	0.515789	0.498669	0.482253
5	0.593451	0.567427	0.542760	0.519369	0.497177	0.476113	0.456111	0.437109	0.419049	0.401878
6	0.534641	0.506631	0.480319	0.455587	0.432328	0.410442	0.389839	0.370432	0.352142	0.334898
7	0.481658	0.452349	0.425061	0.399637	0.375937	0.353830	0.333195	0.313925	0.295918	0.279082
8	0.433926	0.403883	0.376160	0.350559	0.326902	0.305025	0.284782	0.266038	0.248671	0.232568
9	0.390925	0.360610	0.332885	0.307508	0.284262	0.262953	0.243404	0.225456	0.208967	0.193807
10	0.352184	0.321973	0.294588	0.269744	0.247185	0.226684	0.208037	0.191064	0.175602	0.161506

Glossary |

accruals: An accrual is where you recognise a charge for some goods or service that you have used but for which you have not as yet received an invoice (e.g., the quarterly telephone account, where you make calls each month but receive a bill only quarterly and in arrears).

acid test (or quick ratio): A measure of business liquidity that shows a business's ability to pay its bills on time. A refinement of the current ratio, it takes into account only those liquid assets that a business holds and compares these with all the current liabilities. It can be calculated as follows, and is shown as a ratio to 1:

Acid test = current assets (excluding all stocks) : current liabilities

asset-based financing: A funding facility designed to provide working capital to fast-growing businesses. The two main types of asset-based financing are factoring and invoice discounting, and stock finance. Cash is advanced against debtors and stock so that as these grow more cash is available to the business.

asset turn: Asset turn measures how many £s of sales each £ of fixed assets generates. Its purpose is to show how efficiently a business is using its fixed assets. The principle is that the higher the value of sales that each fixed asset is generating the better. You may have heard the expression 'sweating your assets' – this is what it means. It is calculated as follows:

$$\text{Asset turn} = \frac{\text{Sales}}{\text{Fixed assets @ NBV}}$$

average rate of return (ARR): By far and away the simplest way of evaluating a capital project is to measure the average profit it generates over its life and express this as an average – average rate of return. It is calculated as follows:

$$ARR = \frac{\text{Average return}}{\text{Cost of investment}}$$

balance sheet: A 'snapshot' of the business at a point in time (usually the financial year end) showing:

- where the business got its money from (usually shareholders and loans, known as liabilities)
- where the business spent it (usually things it uses in the business, known as assets)
- the time perspective for each of these – either short-term or long-term

break-even point (BEP): The point at which total sales cover all total costs and the business makes neither profit nor loss. It can be calculated as follows:

$$\text{Break-even point (BEP)} = \frac{\text{Fixed costs}}{\text{Gross margin \%}}$$

break-even profit point (BEPP): The amount of sales needed (target) to achieve the profit objective set by the business. It can be calculated as follows:

$$£\,\text{Sales target (BEPP)} = \frac{\text{Fixed cost + profit objective}}{\text{Gross margin \%}}$$

business angels: Usually high-worth individuals who make equity (shares purchase) investments in businesses. Quite frequently as well as money they can bring valuable skills and contacts to a business. They operate quite informally either on their own (so they are difficult to find) or through business-angel networks. In most respects they operate in the same way as venture-capital firms – investments are made primarily for financial gain.

cash flow forecast: Provides a prediction of how well a business will generate cash and the effect it will have on the bank balance for the forecast period (not necessarily a year). The key features of the cash flow forecast are:

- It shows cash inflow and outflow into a business (usually on a monthly basis).
- It does not distinguish between revenue and capital.
- Its objective is to show the months in which cash flows lead to the bank balance becoming negative and when it returns to a steady state.

circulation of working capital: Measures how efficiently working capital (net current assets) is being used to support the sales of the business. The greater the number of times working capital is being turned the better. It is calculated as follows:

$$\text{Circulation of working capital} = \frac{\text{Sales}}{\text{Net current assets}} \text{ times}$$

creditor days: A measure of how well a business is managing its supplier payments. This measure shows on average how many days it takes to pay your suppliers. The higher this figure the more you are squeezing your suppliers. It is calculated as follows:

$$\text{Creditor days} = \frac{\text{Creditors}}{\text{Cost of sales}} \times 365 \text{ days}$$

creditor strain: Apparent when a business takes too long to pay its creditors and they withdraw all credit facilities. Suddenly the business is faced with having to find additional funding to replace these – usually from their bank. See FAQ 7 for more on creditor strain.

current ratio: Expresses current assets as a ratio to current liabilities. It is used to indicate whether there are sufficient short-term assets to meet the short-term liabilities. It can be calculated as follows, and is shown as a ratio to 1:

$$\text{Current ratio} = \text{Current assets : current liabilities}$$

debenture: A bond, acknowledging a loan to the company, that bears a fixed rate of interest. This interest is payable regardless of whether profits are made or not (unlike shares). The debenture can either be redeemable (at some future agreed date) or irredeemable, in which case redemption will take place only when the company is eventually liquidated. To increase the level of security to the lender under a debenture a charge may be granted over all or certain assets to a debenture holder – known as a mortgage debenture.

debtor days: A measure of how efficiently a business collects the money due to it from its customers (debtors). This measure shows on average how many days it takes to collect your outstanding debts. The higher this figure the more inefficient is your debtor collection process. It is calculated as follows:

$$\text{Debtor days} = \frac{\text{Debtors}}{\text{Sales}} \times 365 \text{ days}$$

discounted cash flow (DCF): DCF attempts to convert cash flows from several different years into cash flows of common value. It does this by applying an agreed present-value factor (PVF) to the cash flows in each year to discount them back to a net present value (NPV) – i.e. today's value. It is calculated as follows:

$$\text{NPV} = \text{Sum of (net cash flows for each year} \times \\ \text{present value factor for each year)}$$

equity: Risk funding provided by shareholders. Their expectation is that as the business becomes more profitable they will receive dividends and their shares will increase in value. In hard times, when the company make little or no profit, they will receive no dividends and their shares will go down in value.

factoring: Using this, the business 'sells' its invoices to a factor (usually part of a bank) and contracts its sales ledger administration to the factor. This can include full bad-debt protection (called non-recourse factoring) or exclude bad-debt cover (recourse factoring). The former is more expensive because it covers an element of bad-debt insurance, so that the factor cannot have any comeback (recourse) against the business if the debt goes bad. Usually available for businesses achieving or forecasting turnover of around £100,000 + per annum.

fixed costs: Are, as the name suggests, the remaining costs that do not vary with sales, i.e. if one extra sale is made no more of this type of cost is incurred. Typical examples of fixed costs are rent, rates, insurance, administration salaries etc.

gearing: Measures how much of the long-term capital in the business has been provided by means of debt and is expressed as a percentage (e.g., 20 per cent). Borrowed money (debt) is regarded as risk money because it must be repaid (with interest) even if the business is loss. Gearing below 50 per cent is preferable to show that the business is not too dependent on borrowed money. This also leaves further scope for borrowing if the business needs it later. Should be used in conjunction with interest cover. It is calculated as follows:

$$\text{Gearing percentage} = \frac{\text{Creditors (due after 12 months)} + \text{bank overdraft}}{\text{Shareholders' funds} + \text{creditors (due after 12 months)} + \text{bank overdraft}} \times 100$$

goodwill: The difference between what you pay for a business over and above the value of the net assets. In effect, it is the amount that you have paid 'over the odds' to buy that business. Accounting standards demand that it should be written off as quickly as possible against available profits.

grants and awards: There are a series of grants available to businesses in selected regions (Regional Selective Assistance (RSA)) and via the Rural Development Commission (RDC). Other support is aimed specifically at businesses involved in innovation and technology (e.g., SMART Award, SPUR Award, TCS (Teaching Company Scheme)). (See FAQ 23.)

gross-profit-to-sales percentage (GP per cent): Gross profit is what is left of the sales revenue after all the variable costs have been taken off. Many observers regard gross profit (or gross profit percentage) as the most important measure of business performance because it represents the 'real' income of the business. GP per cent expresses gross profit as a percentage of sales to measure the margin made from each £ of sales made. It is calculated as follows:

$$\text{Gross profit percentage (GP per cent)} = \frac{\text{Gross profit}}{\text{Sales}} \times 100$$

hire purchase (HP): Under an HP agreement the business is contracting to buy the asset over an agreed period of years. To this extent it is similar to a term loan except that the rate of interest paid will usually be higher and there will be penalties for early repayment of the loan. At the end of the HP contract the asset belongs to the business.

interest cover: Measures the ability of the business to meet the interest payments out of profit, expressed as number (e.g., five times). Should be used in conjunction with gearing

It is calculated as follows:

$$\text{Interest cover} = \frac{\text{Operating profit}}{\text{Bank and loan interest}} \text{ times}$$

invoice discounting: Using this, the business exchanges sales invoices for cash, but retains full control over its own invoicing and debtor collection. However, bad-debt protection can be provided as part of this package. Invoice discounting will usually be the cheaper form of debtor financing if no other service is being used. Usually available for businesses achieving or forecasting turnover of around £750,000 + (with no upper limit).

leasing and contract hire: Under a lease or contract hire the business contracts to rent (not own) the asset over an agreed period of time – usually its useful life. It is responsible for maintaining the asset and returning it in good condition at the end of the period. There are penalties for early cancellation of the contract and at its end the asset will usually be required to be returned to its owner.

margin of safety: The amount that sales can safely drop before all the profits of the business are wiped out (i.e., break-even point is reached). A critical measure of vulnerability in a business. Any business with a margin of safety of less than 20 per cent is unlikely to survive a recession.

net profit after tax to sales (net-profit-after-tax percentage): The net-profit-after-tax percentage expresses net profit after tax (PAT) as a percentage of sales. Shows how profitable a business is after all business costs (trading and financing) and after it has allowed for tax. It gives some measure of how much profit will be available for giving to the shareholders (dividends) and how much, if any, will be left for future growth and development of the business. It is calculated as follows:

$$\text{Net-profit-after-tax percentage} = \frac{\text{Net profit after tax}}{\text{Sales}} \times 100$$

operating profit to sales (operating-profit percentage): The operating-profit percentage expresses operating profit (sometimes also known as trading profit) as a percentage of sales. Shows how profitable the business is after all operating (or trading) expenses but before any financing costs (bank interest etc.). Operating-profit percentage falls between GP per cent and net-profit-after-tax percentage. It is calculated as follows:

$$\text{Operating profit percentage} = \frac{\text{Operating profit}}{\text{Sales}} \times 100$$

overtrading: This term is used to explain the situation in which a business is growing beyond its ability to generate or get additional working capital

payback period: Has become the most popular method for evaluating capital projects. It compares the initial cash cost of the investment with the subsequent cash inflows to determine how many years it takes to pay back the cost of the investment. It is calculated as follows:

$$\text{Payback} = \frac{\text{Total net cash flows}}{\text{Cost of investment}}$$

prepayments: Prepayment is where you pay in advance for some goods or service that you have not used (e.g., the quarterly telephone account, where you pay in advance for the next quarter's line rental).

price/earnings (P/E) ratio: A multiple of profits used to value a business (e.g., value of business = 12 × net profit). The P/E or multiple will vary according to industry sector depending on the maturity of the sector. As an example for a mature and established sector, such as construction, the appropriate P/E may be as low as 5. On the other hand, for a new and dynamic sector, such as Internet retailing, the appropriate P/E may be infinite (in the case of new businesses) and 30+ in the case of young businesses.

profitability index (PI): The profitability index takes DCF a stage further by providing a comparison between projects that have identical NPVs but have different capital investment values – a sort of 'tie breaker'. It is calculated as follows:

$$\text{Profitability index (PI)} = \frac{\text{Net present value (NPV)}}{\text{Cost of investment}} \times 100$$

profit growth: Shows year-on-year growth in net profit after tax (PAT), expressed as a percentage. Used to show how 'bottom-line' profit is being maintained against sales over the last twelve months. It is calculated as follows:

$$\text{Profit after growth percentage} = \frac{\text{This year's PAT} - \text{last year's PAT}}{\text{Last year's PAT}} \times 100$$

profit per employee: Probably not as useful as sales per employee in measuring pure people performance since most of the business costs are not people-related. However, this measure can be used to evaluate how much profit each person helps to create after the full business costs. It is calculated as follows:

$$\text{Profit per employee (£)} = \frac{£ \, \text{Net profit after tax (PAT)}}{\text{Number of employees}}$$

'quick' profit report: A cheap (free) and cheerful (simple) way of quickly calculating the net profit for a business using the principles of break-even and margin of safety. Using just three real (or estimated) figures you can calculate, monitor and project the net profit for a business.

ratchet: A mechanism used by venture capitalists to incentivise the management of a company where they have made an equity investment. In effect, it enables the management to acquire additional shares at no cash cost to them in exchange for exceeding projected profits. Works on the basis that if the management increase the profits of the business it will be worth more when it is sold – so the venture capitalist is prepared to share excess value with the management (not in cash but in shares).

ratio analysis: The use of ratios (or key financial relationships) to evaluate a business's performance over periods of time, to establish trends, or against competitors, to establish comparative performance. Using this approach the management can identify where business performance is poor (e.g., poor debtor collection highlighted by rise in debtor-days ratio) and focus effort to improve it.

return on capital employed (ROCE): Expresses operating profit as a percentage of capital employed. Shows how much profit (or return) is available to all the providers of the long-term capital (shareholders and long term creditors). If this return is high it indicates that the business will be able to attract additional funding if needed. Conversely, if it is low (below other similar investments), then the business will be unable to attract any additional funding. It is calculated as follows:

$$\text{ROCE percentage} = \frac{\text{Operating profit}}{\text{Capital employed}} \times 100$$

return on shareholders' capital (ROSC): The return-on-shareholders'-capital percentage (ROSC per cent) expresses net profit after tax as a percentage of shareholders' capital (capital and reserves). Shows how much profit (or return) is available to the shareholders (just one group of providers of the long-term capital). If this return is high it indicates that the business will be able to attract additional funding if needed. Conversely, if it is low (below bank base rate), then the business will be unable to attract any additional funding. It is calculated as follows:

$$\text{ROSC percentage} = \frac{\text{Net profit after tax}}{\text{Capital and reserves}} \times 100$$

sales growth: Shows year-on-year growth in sales, expressed as a percentage. Used to show if your business has grown over the last twelve months and by how much. It is calculated as follows:

$$\text{Sales growth percentage} = \frac{\text{This year's sales} - \text{last year's sales}}{\text{Last year's sales}} \times 100$$

sales per employee: Shows improvement in sales revenue generated by each employee. Can be used as a justification for employing more staff (if it is increasing). Conversely, it can be used to reduce staff levels if the figure is very low or falling. It is calculated as follows:

$$\text{Sales per employee } (\pounds) = \frac{\pounds \text{ Sales}}{\text{Number of employees}}$$

Small Firms Loan Guarantee Scheme: A loan arranged with a bank in the traditional way, but under this scheme the Department of Trade and Industry (DTI) guarantee it. It is available for loans from £5,000 to £250,000 over periods of two to ten years and for most business purposes. The DTI will guarantee to pay the lending bank up to 85 per cent of the outstanding loan if the borrower fails to repay. It is specifically for businesses that have a good business proposition but do not have security to cover the loan – which is why the bank will do it only under this scheme.

stock finance: Using this the business makes its stock available as part of an 'all-inclusive deal' with factoring or invoice discounting to increase the amount of cash available against its sales invoices. This is in effect the sweetener to uplift the 80 per cent advance to 100 per cent of sales.

stock turn: Measures how efficiently a business converts its stock into sales. This measure shows how many times a year stock is 'turned over' or sold – the higher this figure the better. The sole purpose of carrying stock is to sell it (as quickly as possible) for as much as possible (GP per cent). Therefore, the longer it remains unsold the more it costs in lost (or paid) bank interest and delayed profit. It is calculated as follows:

$$\text{Stock turn} = \frac{\text{Cost of sales}}{\text{All stocks}} \text{ times a year}$$

value added per employee (VAPE): Shows how much 'gross contribution' each employee has made. In effect it shows how much 'real' income they have brought in (gross profit) to cover their remuneration and contribute to profit. Used to highlight the efficiency in the use of people in the business especially if related to average remuneration. It is calculated as follows:

$$\text{VAPE } (\pounds) = \frac{\pounds \text{ Sales} - (\text{materials} + \text{bought-in services in cost of sales})}{\text{Number of employees}}$$

variable costs: As their name suggests, these are all those costs that vary with sales (i.e., for each extra sale that is made some more of this type of cost must be incurred). Typical examples of variable costs are materials, direct labour (those people who make the product or service), sales commission (because it is based on sales made).

venture capitalist: A specialist business that provides risk capital to limited companies. They do this by buying equity (shares) in a company. Venture capitalists have their own sector specialities and stages of company development that they prefer to invest at.

warranty: A warranty can be defined as a statement made in a contract that, if unfulfilled, does not usually invalidate the contract but could lead to the payment of damages. If the warranty is clearly stated in writing it is known as an express warranty and if it is not but is understood by both parties it is known as an implied warranty.

working capital: Also known as net current assets. The short-term assets (debtors, stock, work in progress) less liabilities (trade creditors and bank overdraft) of a business. Shows the day-to-day funding requirement of a business.

CENTRE FOR SMALL & MEDIUM SIZED ENTERPRISES

Warwick is one of a handful of European business schools that have won a truly global reputation. Its high standards of both teaching and research are regularly confirmed by independent ratings and assessments.

The Centre for Small & Medium Sized Enterprises (CSME) is one of the school's major research centres. We have been working with people starting a business, or already running one, since 1985. The Centre also helps established companies to reignite the entrepreneurial flame that is essential for any modern business.

We don't tell entrepreneurs what to do – just help them be more aware and better informed of the opportunities and pitfalls of running a growing small enterprise.

Much of our practical knowledge is gleaned from the experience of individuals who themselves have been there and done it. These kinds of business coaches rarely commit their observations to paper, but in this Virgin/Warwick series they have captured in print their passion and their knowledge. It's a new kind of business publishing that addresses the constantly evolving challenge of business today.

For more information about Warwick Business School (courses, owner networks and other support to entrepreneurs, managers and new enterprises), please contact:

Centre for Small & Medium Sized Enterprises
Warwick Business School
University of Warwick
Coventry CV4 7AL
UK
Tel: +44 (0) 2476 523741 (CSME); or 524306 (WBS)
Fax: +44 (0) 2476 523747 (CSME); or 523719 (WBS)
Email: enquiries@wbs.warwick.ac.uk
And visit the Virgin/CSME pages via:
www.wbs.warwick.ac.uk

Also available in the Virgin Business Guides series:

LITTLE e, BIG COMMERCE
HOW TO MAKE A PROFIT ONLINE

Timothy Cumming

Now that the first wave of dotcom mania has passed, the right way to run a website is becoming clearer. If you haven't taken the e-Commerce plunge yet, or if you want to get more out of your website, we'll introduce you to the world of e-customers, e-competitors and e-suppliers, taking you through the practical steps of getting and staying online. You'll find out what e-Commerce really is and how to do it properly – and, above all, profitably – so you can make money instead of draining your resources. With the expert advice in this book, you can stay ahead of this fast-moving game.

ISBN 0 7535 0542 8

KICK-START YOUR BUSINESS
100 DAYS TO A LEANER, FITTER ORGANISATION

Robert Craven

Feel your business could do with a tune-up, but are too busy running it to sort out the problems? With the fast, proven techniques in this book, you can transform your workplace into a powerhouse. The case studies, worksheets and practical exercises will help you to take the pain out of business planning, increase your profitability and keep your customers. You'll find out how to identify your company's strengths and weaknesses and assess its potential, and learn the secret obsessions of all successful entrepreneurs.

ISBN 0 7535 0532 0

THE BEST-LAID BUSINESS PLANS
HOW TO WRITE THEM, HOW TO PITCH THEM

Paul Barrow

Planning is not just for start-ups – it's the key to successful business development and growth for every company, new or old. But once a business is up and running, it's all too easy to concentrate only on day-to-day operations. If you're launching new products and services, taking on more people, relocating to bigger premises, buying a business or selling one, you'll do it better if you plan it. This book shows you how to present the right plan for the right audience – so you stand a better chance of getting what you need. The sound practical advice, case studies and exercises in this book will help you through the planning process and ensure that yours are indeed the best-laid plans.

ISBN 0 7535 0537 1

DO SOMETHING DIFFERENT
PROVEN MARKETING TECHNIQUES TO
TRANSFORM YOUR BUSINESS

Jurgen Wolff

If you carry on doing what you've been doing, you're going to carry on getting to where you've been getting. So if you want more business, you'd better *Do Something Different!* This book, built around 100 instructive and revealing case studies, contains plenty of advice on how to take charge of your situation and create your own alternatives. It's full of examples of entrepreneurs who took a sideways look at the market and their competitors, and decided to branch out and do something a little bit surprising. As a result they made their products and their companies stand out among the competition – vital in today's business environment. Engagingly written by a great individualist, *Do Something Different* will show you how to break the mould and find your way to greater success. Follow its advice and you can set yourself apart from the crowd.

ISBN 0 7535 0528 2

IT'S NOT ABOUT SIZE
BIGGER BRANDS FOR SMALLER BUSINESSES

Paul Dickinson

Branding is one of the most important aspects of marketing for any enterprise. In this straightforward guide, Paul Dickinson, who has worked to define some of the biggest brands in the world, shows how an eye for detail and design can help to re-energise any company or organisation. In this book, you'll find out how simple brand identifiers like colour and 'feel' can make powerful statements about your company, no matter what its size. Paul Dickinson shows how to change the way you think about your company's identity, and how to take simple steps to increase your sales and profits through effective branding and enhanced customer satisfaction. Fascinating case studies demonstrate how the theory has been turned into practical steps – and checklists and action plans will enable you to do the same.

ISBN 0 7535 0593 2